THE DEATH OF BLACK AMERICA

ERAN REYA

AuthorHouse™
1663 Liberty Drive, Suite 200
Bloomington, IN 47403
www.authorhouse.com
Phone: 1-800-839-8640

© *2007 Three Circle, LLC. All rights reserved.*

No part of this book may be reproduced, stored in a retrieval system, or transmitted by any means without the written permission of the author.

First published by AuthorHouse 7/12/2007

ISBN: 978-1-4259-8922-4 (sc)

Library of Congress Control Number: 2007902689

Printed in the United States of America
Bloomington, Indiana

This book is printed on acid-free paper.

Photo cover content provided by
OLD PHOTOGRAPHS OF AFRICAN AMERICANS- UNKNOWN FACES
@ http://www.freewebs.com/opoaa2/

TABLE OF CONTENTS

THE DEATH OF BLACK AMERICA	1
Programming By Trauma	9
Jim Crow	17
False Consciousness And The Parameters Of Blackness	21
We're Not Like The Others	24
What Is Black Culture?	29
THE ARRESTED DEVELOPMENT OF THE BLACK FEMALE	35
The Modern Jezebel/sapphire Persona	43
Carnal Intuition And Male Archetypes	48
Masochism	52
White Feminisim	53
The Pecola Complex	54
Big Mamas & Male Archetypes	55
Zero To Negative Population Growth	57
THE ARRESTED DEVELOPMENT OF THE BLACK MALE	61
The Stud Nigger Persona & Misogyny	72
The Feminist Male	82
Black Male Sexual Identity And Homosexuality	84
Replacing Archetypes & Redefining Manhood	88
CONSPICIOUS CONSUMPTION	91
The Quest For Respect	98
Cannibal Economics And Racial Gatekeepers	102
An Aversion To Learning	106
Conclusion	109

A SPIRITUAL EXODUS 113
    White Divinity 116
    Benevolent Masters 120
    The Complicity Of The White Population 121
    Modern Benevolent Masters 123
    The Pity Party 128
    Spiritual Slaves 131
    Wandering In A Spiritual Wilderness 134

ENDNOTES 141

Holy Bible LUKE 5:36-39

³⁶And he spake also a parable unto them; No man putteth a piece of a new garment upon an old; if otherwise, then both the new maketh a rent, and the piece that was taken out of the new agreeth not with the old. ³⁷And no man putteth new wine into old bottles; else the new wine will burst the bottles, and be spilled, and the bottles shall perish. ³⁸But new wine must be put into new bottles; and both are preserved. ³⁹No man also having drunk old wine straightway desireth new: for he saith, The old is better.

THE DEATH OF BLACK AMERICA

- 70% of African-Americans do NOT live below the poverty line.

- 61% of middle-class Blacks own stock.

- 40% live in suburban neighborhoods.

- ½ trillion dollars a year generated and circulated.

- Several named as wealthiest individuals in the nation.

- Black households earning over $100,000/yr. increased tenfold since 1960's.

- 39 Black members of Congress - 8 times as many as 1964.

- More than ½ of 50 states, including Washington D.C., have Black mayors.

- Blacks are directors of major corporations, university presidents, astronauts, political leaders and military generals. (1)

Amid all of this progress, the Black community is in the midst of a complete social breakdown and population die-off. Since the 1960s, successive generations have been reared without morals, and without a reference to their past. This created a social and cultural vacuum; now filled with consumerism, sexism, and racism. As a consequence, children are now raised without predetermined codes of behavior or boundaries. Without a true social structure, the young have essentially raised themselves. But all people, especially the young, have a need to find meaning and purpose in their lives. In this quest for meaning, we have left the young to appropriate images and ideas fed to them from their surroundings. Black America's young, with no connection to their past, have inadvertently embraced racial stereotypes under the belief that they have built a new social order. The resurrection of the worst aspects of Black America falls squarely at the feet of the Black baby boomer generation. Historian Carroll Quigley wrote:

> The real value of any society rests in its ability to develop mature and responsible individuals prepared to stand on their own feet, make decisions, and be prepared to accept the consequences of their decisions and actions without whining or self-justification. (2)

In March 2006, the Washington Post published an article entitled, "Marriage Is for White People." The author discussed reasons for the decrease in marriage rates among Black Americans. What was most damning was her discussion with sixth grade boys who said they did not want to marry, but would father and take care of a child. The boys agreed that marriage is for White people. (3) We have taught successive generations that nuclear families are not necessary. Forty plus years after the Civil Rights era, we now have generations of children that do not know what a nuclear family looks like. These children are the culmination of over 40 years of economic and social entrance into the American mainstream. It shows Black America's inability to form permanent family structures, rear socially adjusted, independent children, and maintain their own community.

In March 1965, Patrick Daniel Moynihan published a report on the state of the Black masses entitled, "The Negro Family: The Case for National Action." In his report, he outlined the causes of social breakdown within the Black community. He noted that twenty-five percent of all Black households were female headed, twenty-five percent of all Black children were born out of wedlock, and that Black males were largely alienated from family life. (4) Since then, the destructive behaviors that Moynihan warned of have been passed on to future generations. Not having been properly addressed, the Black family has further disintegrated.

- Today, 40 years after the Civil Rights Act of 1964, married couples had only 46% of families.(5)

- In 1970, just 33% of Black women, age 20-29 were unmarried. By 1992, that number exploded to 70% (6)

- 43% of all Black children are aborted, nearly three times higher than Whites. (7)

- According to the Center for Disease Control statistics, 1,500 Black babies are aborted each day in the United States. That amounts to more than 500,000 children per year out of a community that already faces challenges for survival. (8)

- 70% of all Black children are born out of wedlock. (9)

- 62% of Black families with children are headed by a single parent. (10)

- 49% of the 1.2 million Americans living with HIV or AIDS are Black. (11)

- Black women account for 67% of American women with AIDS. (12)

It seems that Black baby boomers believed that Civil Rights legislation and its enforcement would change perceptions and that the racial conflict of the past would be water under the bridge. They could now explore the other side of the fence that segregation had made look so much greener. They fled their communities, took corporate and government jobs, dropped their kids off in formerly White-only schools and daycare, and set about acquiring the good life. They believed that work and social association with White America would uplift the race as a whole. In this process, they began to distance themselves from the past, the painful memories of segregation, and the feelings of inferiority associated with Black American culture. This is the great forgetting. In this transition, they found the traditional underpinnings of the Black community, nuclear families, spirituality, and extended family structures passé. Black boomers made a conscious decision to discourage cultural transference between generation X and pre Civil Rights era Blacks, the grandparents. This great forgetting was intended to prevent successive generations from carrying forward the culture and behaviors associated with their parents.

The baby boomers sought to replace old memories with new ideals based on total assimilation. The problem is that America will never be ready for total assimilation. Legislation outlawed overt racism, but could not change a person's way of thinking, which still closely follows the mindset of Jim Crow. The great forgetting left future Black Americans without the tools necessary to deal with passive-aggressive racism, nor were they equipped to counter preconceived notions of Black inferiority and behavior. Black boomers did not realize that White America is not ready to deal with Black Americans as human beings. White America still perceives Blacks through the lens of history, which they still celebrate as America's heyday. These preconceived ideals of what it means to be a Black American are based in a historical context of innate inferiority. Black children without a past, constantly bombarded with modern images, are now a lost generation awash in moral relativism. Moral relativism is the position that moral or ethical propositions do not reflect absolute and universal moral truths, but instead make claims relative to social, cultural, historical or personal circumstances. (13) Moral relativism was brought to the forefront of American culture in the 1960s. It essentially means do what you feel when you feel it. In the American south, moral relativism and the associated hypocrisy of southern culture was the norm, based on generations of American Christianity and white supremacy. When you produce children with "Moral Relativism," you are a dead community. With ever changing morals and little guidance or social stability, Black America has descended into a group that no longer nurtures the basic unit necessary for survival, healthy heterosexual nuclear families.

    Black America has been given the opportunity to do for self, but we seem to have little self-confidence or initiative. As of 2007, we still look to White America, a people that deemed us 3/5 of a human being, for a means of support. This idea was demonstrated after hurricane Katrina, with the abandonment at the Superdome and the blocked bridge to Gretna, Louisiana incidents. (14) Black America seemed surprised to be abandoned by federal, state, and local governments. This betrayal stings, yet the Black community still seeks concessions and acceptance from a larger community that despises them.

Katrina simply reminded us of our place in American society and that we can not depend upon federal, state, and local government for our survival. But this is exactly what we've allowed to happen since the Civil Rights Act was passed. We've accepted public housing, food stamps, education vouchers, and some entrance into Federal and State employment, but have slipped from a people on the rise, to a people on the edge of the abyss. We assumed our former masters had suddenly turned benevolent and forgot how to do for self. We can no longer shout that the White man has it in for us. The actions of the present day Black community would make Hitler, the KKK, and Margaret Sanger proud. These individuals and White supremacy groups referred to people of color as degenerate mud people, useless eaters that leech off of a well-planned system built by far-thinking White people. We obediently fulfill the goals of people that loath our very existence. Rev. Janine Simpson wrote in her article, "The Urban Initiative," about devout eugenicist, Margaret Sanger:

> Minority communities have long been targeted by eugenicists. Margaret Sanger was a lifelong advocate for increasing access to birth control. To promote this goal, she began publishing the magazine Birth Control Review in 1917 and founded the Birth Control League in 1922. That organization would later change its name to Planned Parenthood. Some revisionist historians laud Margaret Sanger as a great social reformer and attribute to her only the best of motives. They want us to believe that Sanger promoted birth control because of her great compassion for women and minorities who had limited access to contraception.

In truth, Margaret Sanger was an adamant proponent of eugenics. This so-called science postulates that some races are genetically superior and, hence, more fit for survival than others. According to eugenics, the overall fitness of humankind will be enhanced when people with "good" genes reproduce and people with "bad" genes don't. Eugenics is the twisted philosophy that drove Hitler and the Nazis to exterminate six million Jews. Margaret Sanger's writings are laced with her racist views. In her 1922 book, Pivot of Civilization, Sanger promoted birth control as the best means of improving the genetic stock of mankind. In this book, she specifically calls for the segregation of "morons, misfits, and the maladjusted" and for the sterilization of "genetically inferior races". (15) Sanger described her utopian view of a master race:

Let us conceive for the moment at least, a world not burdened by the weight of dependent and delinquent classes, a total population of mature, intelligent, critical and expressive men and women. Instead of the inert, exploitable, mentally passive class which now forms the barren substratum of civilization, try to imagine a population of active, resistant, passing individuals and social lives of the most contented and healthy sort. (16)

In addition to her own writings, Sanger frequently featured articles in her magazine from other well-known eugenicists and racists. For example, one article contributed by well-known Nazi supporter Lothrop Stoddard was entitled, "The Rising Tide of Color against White World Supremacy." Sanger also elected Stoddard to serve on the board of her organization. In 1939, Sanger and her organization launched the Negro Project. Through this project, Sanger sought to convert her philosophical views into public policy. The Negro Project was designed to build clinics in poor communities so birth control would be made available to keep down the rising Black population. To justify this initiative, Sanger explained, "the poorer areas, particularly in the South… are producing alarmingly more than their share of future generations." According to Sanger, birth control would "ease the financial load of caring for with public funds… children destined to become a burden to themselves, to their family, and ultimately to the nation."

Sadly, Sanger persuaded many prominent Black leaders that this promotion of birth control in the Black community was a sound policy. She shrewdly convinced men like W.E.B Dubois and Dr. Clayton Powell that reducing the numbers of African-Americans would cause the quality of life to rise for the remaining members of the community. Nevertheless, Sanger remained concerned that people in the African-American community might learn about her real racist views. In a letter to a colleague, she confided that steps must be taken to keep these views from being known:

"We do not want the word to go out that we want to exterminate the Negro population, and the minister is the man who can straighten out that idea if it ever occurs to one of their more rebellious members." (17)

The self hatred that the Black community executes on itself ensures that we will die out. Richard Delgado refers to Antonio Gramsci's "False Consciousness" to describe this self hatred:

> Gramsci coined the term to mean the kind of identification with the aggressor that a subjugated people can easily develop. They internalize the perspectives, values, and points of view of the very people who conquered and are oppressing them, thus becoming unconscious agents in their own oppression." (18)

We have received the outward appearance of economic and social integration, but the collective psyche and heart of Black America is in need of serious change.

The problem of the twenty first century is the spiritual problem of internalized inferiority, of "false consciousness," about which John C. McWhorter wrote:

> Centuries of abasement and marginalization led African Americans to internalize the way they were perceived by the larger society, resulting in a post-colonial inferiority complex."(19)

PROGRAMMING BY TRAUMA

This inferiority complex is a direct result of white supremacy. In order to have a society based on inequality, one part of society must believe they are unequal or there is constant rebellion against the social order. This social order could only be implemented and maintained through the application of violent physical trauma. The maintenance and perpetuation of White supremacy is the mainstay of southern American culture. John Howard Griffin wrote in "Black Like Me":

> No one, not even a saint, can live without a sense of personal value. The White racist has masterfully defrauded the Negro of this sense. It is the least obvious but most heinous of all race crimes, for it kills the spirit and the will to live. (20)

What does it mean to be a Black American? The Black American is a White American creation. Black Americans would be best described as any Black person whose roots existed in America prior to 1964. Africans, Caribbean Blacks, and Spanish speaking Blacks were not allowed in America until after 1964. They therefore do not have a psychological tie to the social order that created the Black American.

Black Americans are a unique group of people who have derived much of their identity as a result of the trauma programming associated with slavery. The Black American is different than every other African group transferred to the western hemisphere because of the total replacement of identity that occurred through slavery. Stanley Elkins compares slavery in Latin America to American slavery and found more human latitude in the behavior allowed by Latin American slavery versus North American slavery. Elkins wrote:

> He was, true enough, primarily a slave. Yet he might perform multiple roles. He could be a husband and a father (for the American slave these roles had virtually no meaning); open to him also were such activities as artisan, peddler, petty merchant, truck gardeners (the law reserved to him the necessary time and a share of the proceeds, but such arrangements were against the law for sambo); ... These roles were all legitimized and protected outside the

plantation; they offered a diversity of channels for the development of personality. (21)

Even though no modern Black American has any memory of slavery and the degradation involved, slave behavior is still carried on by Black America and is evident in the behavior of the Black community. Stanley Elkins draws striking comparisons of Nazi concentrations camp torture training to the southern plantation system which he describes as:

> The deliberate infliction of various forms of torture upon the incoming prisoners in such a way as to break their resistance and make way for their degradation as individuals. These brutalities were not merely "permitted" or "encouraged"; they were prescribed. (22)

Frederick Douglas was a recipient of such abuse, when as a young man he was sent to a Slave Breaker, a man who specialized in mentally breaking slaves to work. A slave who proved incorrigibly uncooperative or who was a habitual runaway was entrusted by his master to a professional "slave breaker" who, with cow skin whip, branding irons, and other pain-inflicting-instruments, would attempt to transform him into a docile worker. Slave breakers were so efficient in their work that many masters found it expedient to send them their newly acquired slaves in order "to get them off to a good start." (23)

The Nazi SS and guards intentionally sought to destroy any form of disobedience or resistance among the prisoners. It was important to wipe the mental slate clean by destroying all past links to their former identity, so that a new identity could be programmed into the mind of the abused. They had to realize that their old way of thinking would not aid them in their new lives; torture hastened this realization, and therefore, the letting go of their former identity. This abuse brought about what Elkins refers to as a psychic displacement in which he states:

> This experience described as a kind of "splitting of personality," has been noted by most of the inmates who later wrote of their imprisonment. The very extremity of the initial tortures produced in the prisoners what actually amounted to a sense of detachment; these brutalities went so beyond his own experience that they became somehow incredible-they seem to be happening to him but also to someone else. (24)

This psychological detachment was necessary for physical survival. Elkins refers to what Bruno Bettelheim calls a "Subject-object split":

> This subject-object "split" appears to have served a double function; not only was it an immediate psychic defense mechanism against shock, but it also acted as the first thrust toward a new adjustment. (25)

Elkins goes on to describe the "childlike" behavior assumed by prisoners to survive the adjustment to the concentration camp.

> The prisoners developed types of behavior which are characteristic of infancy or early youth. Some of these behaviors developed slowly, others were immediately imposed on the prisoners and developed only in intensity as time went on." (26)

Once the torture victim realized that they had no alternative other than death, they submitted and internalized social standards set by their torturer. The torturer replaced the person's behavior with traits deemed acceptable by him. This new identity is an external construct, and the object must accept this role/identity or die. Elkins refers to Bettelheim's finished product description of prison programming by torture:

> A prisoner had reached the final stage of adjustment to the camp situation when he had changed his personality so as to accept as his own the values of the Gestapo. The old prisoners came to share the attitude of the SS toward the "unfit" prisoners; newcomers who behaved badly in the labor groups or who could not withstand the strain became a liability for the others, who were often instrumental in getting rid of them. Many old prisoners actually imitated the SS; they would sew and mend their uniforms in such a way as to make them look like those of the SS. (27)

This torture and trauma programming of American slavery closely mirrors the Nazi torture program, less the desire for extermination. The concentration camp also followed the same structure as the southern plantation. Officers took the place of southern aristocracy, enlisted guards worked as overseers, and Kapos (trustee prisoners) stood in place of Negro drivers and house slaves who supervised other prisoners and had the ear of their masters. Elkins described the concentration camp hierarchy and the prisoners' assimilation of Nazi ideals as their own:

> These creatures, many of them professional criminals, not only behaved with slavish servility to the

SS, but the way in which they often outdid the SS in sheer brutality became one of the most durable features of the concentration camp legend. (28)

This also explains why the use of the word "nigger" is so common among Black Americans. They have internalized white ideals of Black identity as their own. A slave had to behave within carefully defined parameters. The psychological goal of a slave was to be perpetually dependent upon the master. Elkins wrote about the Nazi prisoners that exhibited this trait:

> To all these men, reduced to complete childlike dependence upon their masters, the SS actually became a father-symbol. (29)

White males had the power of life or death over a slave, and childlike obedience and dependence was the requirement for survival. "Master" and later "Mister" was a title bestowed on any White male over the age of puberty and could command absolute obedience anywhere in the south. Elkins states:

> Absolute power for him meant absolute dependency for the slave-the dependency not of the developing child, but of the perpetual child. For the master, the role most aptly fitting such a relationship would naturally be that of the father. As a father he could be either harsh or kind, as he chose, but as a wise father he would have, we may suspect, a sense of limits of his situation. He must be ready to cope will all the qualities of the child, exasperating as well as the ingratiating. He might conceivably have to expect this child- besides his loyalty, docility, humility, cheerfulness, and (under supervision) his

diligence-such additional qualities as irresponsibility, playfulness, silliness, laziness, and (quite possibly) tendencies to lying and stealing. (30)

Elkins wrote that Nazis initiated behavior modification over only a few years, while American slave behavior was reinforced over generations. He leaves an open ended statement as to the effects of torture/trauma programming over hundreds of years of application:

> If the concentration camp could produce in two or three years the results that it did, one wonders how much more pervasive must have been those attitudes, expectations, and values which had, certainly, their benevolent side and which were accepted and transmitted over generations. (31)

E. Franklin Frazier alludes to this trauma programming as a reflection of the unstable family structure of the Black masses:

> When the sexual taboos and restraints imposed by their original culture were lost, the behavior of slaves in this regard was subject at first only to the control of the masters and the wishes of those selected for mates. Hence, on the large plantations, where slaves were treated almost entirely as instruments of production and brute force was relied upon as the chief means of control, sexual relations were likely to be dissociated on whole from human sentiments and feeling. (32)

Everything that White America despises about the Black American is of their ancestor's making. White America intentionally created its own object of hatred, the "nigger."

This "nigger" identity is the result of torture-induced mind control reinforced over generations. Carter G. Woodson wrote:

> When you control a man's thinking you do not have to worry about his actions. You do not have to tell him not to stand here or go yonder. He will find his "proper place" and will stay in it. You do not need to send him to the back door. He will go without being told. In fact, if there is no door, he will cut one for his special benefit. His education makes it necessary. (33)

During slavery, Blacks were not allowed to choose mates or enter into recognized marriages. This encouraged relationship ambiguity. Any child born of a slave union did not belong to the parents, but to the slave master. Slave unions and informal families were sold apart for financial gain. During slavery, Black relationships were seen by slaveholding America as nothing more than animalist breeding arrangements. Slaveholders did not recognize any boundaries in Black sexuality because that would require that they be regarded as human. The intentional creation of casual sexual/breeding arrangements built the American nigger identity by making slave relationships brief physical encounters. Relationships such as these were forced and commonplace. Slaveholders sought to convince themselves and their slaves that animals do not feel shame. Slaveholders did this to remove any semblance of humanity from Black Americans. Shame in slave communities did not apply to situations one did not have control over, where normal human decorum and boundaries could not be applied. Perhaps over time, exposed to perpetual acts of degradation and shame, those acts can and will become normal and accepted. The removal of shame and the apparent casualness of forced sexual relationships created the mythical hypersexual images of the Black man and Black woman. Once slavery ended, the maintaining of the nigger identity was only possible through the enforcement of federal, state, and local laws until 1964. This alone makes America, for most of its history, a fascist state in which government and business interests colluded to continually dehumanize a segment of its own citizenry. These dehumanizing social rules and laws were called Jim Crow.

JIM CROW

> Jim Crow Laws were state and local laws enacted in the Southern and Border States of the United States and in force between 1876 and 1967 that required racial segregation, especially of Blacks, in all public facilities. (34)

Under Jim Crow, Blacks were denied access to formal education or work in a vocational or white collar profession. Blacks were relegated to physical and menial jobs. Rules for Black behavior and social interaction were very rigid. A Black could not address a White person in proper English, nor look them in the eye. That would suggest that the Black person felt himself equal to the White person and was a threat to White supremacy. If walking down the sidewalk, Blacks were expected to get off the sidewalk to make way for a white person. Stetson Kennedy listed Jim Crow rules for interaction with Whites:

1. Never assert or even intimate that a White person may be lying.

2. Never impute dishonorable intentions to a White person.

3. Never suggest that the White person is of an inferior class.

4. Never lay claim to, or overtly demonstrate, superior knowledge or intelligence.

5. Never curse a White person.

6. Never laugh derisively at a White person.

7. Never comment upon the physical attractiveness of a White person of the opposite sex. (35)

Comedian Michael Richards shouted in November 2006:

"That's what happens when you interrupt the White man, don't you know." (36)

Michael Richards was reinforcing Jim Crow Rule number 4, which states never lay claim to, or overtly demonstrate superior knowledge or intelligence over a white person. Michael Richards was reminding Blacks of their intellectual inferiority and the traditional parameters of white/black social interaction. Many Black Americans have experienced episodes of passive-aggressive racism on all levels of American society. Traditionally, Black intellectual ability is doubted by default, and by tradition any sliver of Black intellectual ability was typically violently squelched by Jim Crow. In slavery and under Jim Crow, any Black person that spoke proper English was described by many as talking "White" and could be harassed for talking on a "White" level of communication. Today the pressure to speak in Ebonics comes from within the Black community.

Some Blacks broke through these parameters of Blackness by working as teachers, doctors, lawyers, and small businessmen. They were thought of by the White community to be racial agitators that gave the masses illusions of equality. These educated Negroes sought a higher standard of living. To the White community, this was a threat to the status quo. For a Negro to realize his own state of wretchedness denoted a mind capable of abstract thought and reason; the opposite of their assigned perpetual state. By tradition, nuclear family, economic independence, education, and culture were things White America discouraged within the Black community. Anything done on par with White America was a threat to the idea of European racial superiority, and the socioeconomic benefits of a controlled, and cheap labor force.

Blacks have accepted this ideology of white superiority and have taught it to successive generations. At present, Blacks generally will not question the intellectual capacity or the decision making of a White person. Making the White person feel inadequate, especially if it is a person in power, can make a Black American's career aspirations very difficult. Any Blacks that outperform White people in areas outside of assumed racial parameters are looked at as aberrations. Many modern White conservatives and liberals alike still believe the racial stereotypes espoused by former U.S. Senator Theodore Bilbo:

> In the skull of the negro [the crania] capacity and the brain itself are much under size. On the average the former will measure thirty-five ounces as against forty-five for the Caucasian skull. In the Negro the cranial bones are dense and unusually thick, converting his head into a veritable battering-ram: moreover, the cranial sutures unite very early in life. This checks the development of the brain long before the same takes place in other races, and this fact accounts to some extent for the more or

less sudden stunting of the Negro intellect shortly after arriving at puberty. (37)

Bilbo goes further and states:

We may say the same thing of his mental and moral qualifications. Professor Keane states that the mental and moral differences between the negro and the White races are quite as well marked as the physical ones, 'and as both are the gradual outcome of external conditions, fixed by heredity, it follows that the attempt to suddenly transform the negro mind by foreign culture must be, as it has proved to be, as futile as the attempt would be to suddenly transform his physical type,'- a point that the untutored masses in the United States fail to see. The Negro has, in fact, no morals, and it is therefore out of the question for him to be immoral; in other words, he is non- moral rather than immoral. (38)

Former Senator Bilbo is taking the idea of Moral Relativism a bit further and says that Blacks innately have no social boundaries. Senator Bilbo's idea of the subhuman as a Black person who is non-moral because he cannot be moral is based in the trauma programming of slavery. To him a Black person is an animal, a beast of the field that follows the urges of the body to eat, sleep, and breed. Again, this points to the "nigger" being a southern American construct. Slaves were forced to live non-moral lives in servitude for generations. Senator Bilbo believed that the limited capacity of the Negro was the reason for the non-moral ways of Negroes. Many Blacks deep in their psyche believe in the inferiority of the Negro mind. If this were not true, we would not see the stifling of intelligence and the disdain for learning among young Black Americans. Modern Black

America has accepted and now glorifies Bilbo's non-moral behaviors called the parameters of Blackness.

FALSE CONSCIOUSNESS AND THE PARAMETERS OF BLACKNESS

The parameters of Blackness fall under Gramsci's definition of false consciousness, but manifest in two ways within the Black populace: one of total shame and aversion by the Black bourgeoisie; the other is the masses acceptance of a permanent state of wretchedness. The more troubling of the two is the situation of the masses. The masses have now embraced a position of innate Black wretchedness, and thus glorify and perpetuate self-destructive behavior in the form of street culture. Professor Beth Richie states:

> Young people today in lower-income Black communities are facing a . . . whole set of stereotypical images of themselves-hypersexual, sexually irresponsible, not concerned with ongoing intimate relationships. They can't help but be influenced by those images. (39)

Black television, music, and film simply reinforce traditional stereotypes that evolved from slavery and Jim Crow. The thug and the Black whore image are nothing more than modern versions of the Black brute and the Jezebel stereotypes initiated by traditional White supremacist ideology. Dr. David Pilgrim wrote about the traditional Jezebel stereotype:

> The Black woman as prostitute, for example, is a staple in mainstream movies, especially those with urban settings. The Black prostitute and the Black pimp supposedly give these movies cutting

edge realism. Small budget pornographic movies reinforce vile sexual stereotypes of Black women. These women are willing, sometimes predatory, sexual deviants who will fulfill any and all sexual fantasies. Their sexual performances tap into centuries-old images of Black women as uninhibited whores. (40)

This image is now standard in most music videos, films, and television, but it is also reinforced from within the community. The Motivational Educational Entertainment survey states:

Even if bravado or "lying on one's dick" may account for some of the tales and blasé attitudes toward this sexual violence, the fact that young women reported it too, along with some admitting to having sex with more than one partner at a time, suggests a disturbing acceptance of the abuse of women. (41)

Dr. David Pilgrim also writes about the brute caricature:

The brute caricature portrays Black men as innately savage, animalistic, destructive, and criminal - - deserving punishment, maybe death. This brute is a fiend, a sociopath, an anti-social menace. Black brutes are depicted as hideous, terrifying predators who target helpless victims, especially White women. (42)

The roles of the whore and the thug are now the norm within the community, and will eventually be passed on to the offspring of people that practice personal relationships in such a way. The normalizing of such dysfunctional gender roles by a community fits the idea of false consciousness. The masses believe what White supremacists have always espoused the Black community to be; a race ruled by innate degenerate behavior and of low spiritual and intellectual capacity. White supremacy during slavery and Jim Crow contrived these stereotypes as a justification for slavery and the restriction of Civil Rights. The Black masses now self impose these images previously forced upon the community through trauma programming.

We no longer have a cohesive Black community to counter this self destructive trend. To be accepted by peers in the Black community, one must fit the parameters of Blackness, which requires a command of Ebonics, athleticism, blatant sexuality, violence, and most of all being "down" with the latest self destructive trends within the community.

Black Americans only have self confidence in those areas that Whites deem the realm of Black Americans. We as a race have taken our collective identity from a people that think us inferior, and teach it to each generation. Anyone that does not act according to the parameters of Blackness is usually ostracized from the community. Black America self–imposes the stereotypes of Jim Crow upon its own by excommunicating members of the community that might contribute to its betterment. Anyone that tries to break out of the parameters of Blackness is said to be acting "White" or a "sellout." This racial peer pressure now results in the degradation of ourselves in a self-imposed Jim Crow society. It appears that some in the community believing that they are "niggers" set out to be the most ignorant bastards possible. This ideology comes from the segregated south and migrated north to the cities carried by people who, looking for a better life, carried the crippling effects of Jim Crow deep in their hearts.

This false consciousness also manifests itself in the use of the word "nigger" by Black Americans. The use of the word nigger by Black Americans and the stereotypical personas associated with it are a weak attempt to appropriate a label meant to deprive the Black community of its humanity. The masses have tried pitifully to turn an externally assigned label into an internally invented identity associated with self-respect. This means that the building blocks of Black American identity are flawed to begin with and should be cast aside for something new. But this has not happened, and we continually try to appropriate every stereotypical label given to us by White America and piece together some twisted sense of self-worth. All the attempts to reclaim the word "nigger" have failed to redefine it and strip it of power. All we have done is reinforce the views of the larger American culture, and kept the legacy of slavery alive and maintained the stifling parameters of Blackness.

WE'RE NOT LIKE THE OTHERS

The Black bourgeoisie, on the other hand, have sought approval and inclusion in mainstream America. They saw themselves as wrongly attached to the masses simply because of their color and set about dispelling the myth of racial inferiority by demonstrations of merit. W.E.B Dubois felt that the problem of bridging the separation of races and how they related to one another was the problem of the twentieth century. In Souls of Black Folks he states:

> The Problem of the Twentieth Century is the problem of the color line. (43)

Alain Locke also wrote about bridging this gap, this color-line between races through merit, a stance which promoted the need for Black America to justify a higher status in mainstream American society. In the essay, "The New Negro," he wrote:

> Our greatest rehabilitation may possibly come through such channels, but for the present, more immediate hope rests in the revaluation by White and Black alike of the Negro in terms of his artistic endowment and cultural contributions, past and prospective. It must be increasingly recognized that the Negro has already made very substantial contributions, not only in his folk-art, music especially, which has always found appreciation, but in larger, though humbler and less acknowledged ways."
> (44)

The Black community believed that if given the chance to demonstrate merit, it would change White America's collective perception of the Negro. The Black bourgeoisie demonstrated false consciousness in their hatred of themselves and their community in that they segregated themselves from the masses. They sought to differentiate themselves from the masses as a distinctly different type of Negro. Carter G. Woodson in his work, "The Mis-Education of the Negro," gives many examples of the Black bourgeoisie's disdain for doing business with other Negroes and uplifting the community in which they live. He wrote:

> Right in the heart of the highly educated Negro section of Washington, too, is a restaurant catering through the front door exclusively to the White business men, who must live in the Negroes' section to supply them with the necessities of life, and catering at the same time through the back door to numbers of Negroes who pile into that dingy room to purchase whatever may be thrown at them. Yet less

than two blocks away are several Negroes running cafés where they can be served for the same amount and under desirable circumstances. (45)

The Black bourgeoisie embraced Americanism and its racist perceptions and ideologies, and segregated themselves within the Black community. Everything they did was to separate themselves from the masses. Their social clubs, vacation spots, arts and entertainment were an imitation of a White mainstream culture. It appears that the Black bourgeoisie has a greater inferiority complex than the masses. They do not feel accepted by mainstream America, but did not embrace the masses. This shame of Blackness, the equating of Blackness with innate inferiority and sin reflects a false consciousness. E. Franklin Frazier wrote:

Having abandoned their social heritage and being rejected by the White world, the Black bourgeoisie have an intense feeling of inferiority, constantly seeking various forms of recognition and place value upon status symbols in order to compensate for their inferiority complex." (46)

The Black bourgeoisie only worked with the masses out of necessity. Civil Rights leader, Robert F. Williams, author of "Negroes with Guns," was abandoned by the NAACP when he battled injustice in Monroe, NC. The NAACP asked him to apologize to White America when he advocated armed defense of the Black community after the White rapist of a pregnant Black woman was acquitted of all charges. (47) This inaction and appeasement further demonstrates the false consciousness in which the Black bourgeoisie sought acceptance at the expense of self-respect. It simply boils down to cowardice and self-loathing. This lack of self-respect explains their attempts to create a separate society within the Black community. It also is reflected in the rhetoric of modern day conservative Blacks as a way to disassociate themselves from the plight of the masses. Frazier wrote:

> The elite who have set themselves apart as Negro "society" and have attempted to maintain an exclusive "social" life, have been extremely conscious of their inferior status in American life. For them "social" life has not only provided a form of participation; it has represented an effort to achieve identification with upper class Whites by imitating as far as possible the behavior of White "society".
> (48)

Today's Black bourgeoisie still holds on to this imitation of White society with its Black debutantes, sorority and fraternal organizations, and social clubs. In some organizations, light skin color and fine hair texture are still highly esteemed. The Black bourgeoisie simply used the masses as cannon fodder to advance desegregation.

The Civil Rights movement boiled down to well-to-do elements in the Black community seeking to be set free from the masses. Under segregation, Blacks were forced to live and work within their own community. Within the community, the Black bourgeoisie consisted of doctors, lawyers, dentists, and educators, and clergy who made their living off of the Black masses.

They wanted the right to shop, vacation, eat, and educate themselves in White-only establishments. During the Bus Boycott in Birmingham, Alabama, Blacks had paid the same fare as Whites, but were not given equal access to the bus. They'd taken this treatment for years. Had it not occurred to anyone before Rosa Parks, to simply not ride the bus? Blacks could have ridden bicycles to work or they could have started their own bus or taxi services. Blacks continually patronize businesses that despise them because of self shame. Rosa Parks gave the Black Bourgeoisie the spark for a movement that initially only benefited a small parasitic upper class that wanted to be free of its host, the Black masses.

After the Voting Rights Act of 1964, the Black bourgeoisie did not turn inward to take advantage of the freedom to do business and grow their communities. They fled to the suburbs to live among White Americans, who promptly sold their homes to escape the onslaught of Negroes that wanted to cozy up to them. Frazier wrote:

> As the system of rigid racial segregation has broken down, the Black bourgeoisie has lost much of its feeling of racial solidarity with the Negro Masses." (49)

Why did the Black bourgeoisie not stay in their own community to educate the Negro masses? Because the Black community has always been one in which individuals want to escape. The color identification of "Black" means less than in the collective American psyche. The Black bourgeoisie followed the same pattern of the house Negroes of slavery and the Kapos of Nazi concentrations camps by seeking release from their racial classification through associations with their superiors. E. Franklin Frazier wrote:

> In escaping from identification with the masses, the Black bourgeoisie has attempted to identify with the White propertied classes. (50)

But today, we have Black bourgeoisie gathering in new Black communities in such places as Washington, D.C., and Atlanta. They have come to realize that White America does not want them; no matter how fine the suit, how nice the car, no matter how articulate they speak, or how advanced the degree. Many in Black America have begun to wonder why they should work so hard to find favor in a group of people that despises them. Seeking to prove that they're not like the others is finally hitting home as a waste of time. Forty years later, we've lost financial ground and grassroots support by population dispersal. But we've also lost our identity.

WHAT IS BLACK CULTURE?

Culture is defined as the behaviors and beliefs of a particular social, ethnic, or age group. Traditionally, Black American culture is shaped by the ability to adjust and adapt to parameters imposed upon it by a larger culture in order to survive. Essentially, we have pieced together a culture from the shreds of what survived our African heritage and the limited expectations of mainstream America. Generally, the masses were continually locked out of mainstream America. Our culture was portable via music and verbal exchange. But the essential element that remained constant was that of maintaining one's humanity amid adversity. The idea of "soul" translates to humanity in Black America.

Soul is defined as the principle of life, feeling, thought, and action in humans, regarded as a distinct entity separate from the body, and commonly held to be separable in existence from the body. It is the spiritual part of humans as distinct from the physical part.

Strong's Concordance defines soul as the two parts of soul called by the Greek word, <u>psuchikos</u>. <u>Psuchikos</u> encompasses both ethereal or spiritual thought and the instinctual motivations of the flesh. This struggle to preserve one's human value in the face of its denial, the internal belief that you are human even when your environment seeks to deny you human dignity, is the essence of being Black American.

The denial of another's humanity is racism. America sought to convince Black America of the lie that Black people are forever outside of God's grace. They sought to create an infinite hell on earth with no hope of redemption or reprieve from this low state called Blackness.

To counter this denial of humanity, of soul, we created our own testament in music, words, and deeds. Field songs and hymns became gospel music that later transformed into blues and jazz. All were acts of defiance; it was the simple refusal to let others define us, the refusal to let others deny us our God given souls.

Black culture today is void of this idea. As a result, we've lost our children. We've let mainstream perceptions and beliefs become Black American beliefs, and the price is our soul. We now embrace the very perceptions that our ancestors sought to destroy. We now have a selfish, sex-crazed culture that mirrors mainstream America, yet is colored by history. Frazier states:

> The folk tradition of the Negro, like the genteel tradition, has been dissipated or transformed as the result of migration and urbanization. (51)

E. Franklin Frazier believed that urbanization due to the great migration further weakened the Black family. The folk culture of the Deep South came north with people who sprung largely from agricultural sharecropping and tenant farming backgrounds that were just a step above slavery. They carried the plantation mindset to the city. The folk culture of the masses was a vestige of slavery. Frazier states:

In their relative isolation they developed a folk culture with its peculiar social organization and social evaluations. Within the world of the Black folk, social relations have developed out of the intimate and sympathetic contacts. Consequently, the maternal-family organization, a heritage from slavery, has continued on a fairly large scale. But the maternal-family organization has also been tied up with the widespread illegitimacy which one still finds in these rural communities. Illegitimacy among these folk is generally a harmless affair, since it does not disrupt the family organization and involves no violation of the mores. Although formal education has done something in the way of dispelling ignorance and superstition, it has effected little change in the mores and customs of these folk communities. (52)

Civility no longer exists in the Black community. We no longer exhibit the regard or respect for others that is essential for a healthy community. With the urbanization of Black culture, we retained the worse aspects of folk culture, yet threw away the idea of extended family via blood relationships and informal adoption. The traditional folk culture could absorb a certain amount of family disorganization because the Black community maintained a certain amount of self sufficiency via subsistence farming and low wage jobs. With the urban migration, this ability to subsist outside of the mainstream no longer existed. Urban living requires living wages in order to maintain a household of any sort. Any disruptions in income reaped havoc on urban households.

During the last waves of the great migration in the late 1940s, many Blacks were barred from gainful employment. Many of the transplants from the south caught the tail end of America's industrial hey-day as many factories were relocating to the suburbs, and later out of America entirely. Without the legitimate sources of employment and revenue, the urban Black culture degenerated into a common gang culture that is now packaged and sold worldwide in the form of rap music of which more than 80% of the consumers are White teenagers.

The war on poverty simply enabled behaviors that as of 1964 affected only about twenty-five percent of the population, but now affect over 65% of the Black American population. Prior to this, the vestiges of slavery remained an undercurrent of the community because of constructive efforts to counter the social, legal, and environmental effects of racism. These efforts were laid aside for economic access and handouts, and the Black community is spiritually and emotionally worse off. These problems came to a head with the crack cocaine epidemic of the 1980s. The crack cocaine epidemic compounded the problems of illegitimacy, child neglect, physical and sexual abuse. Crack cocaine further weakened already stressed, female headed households. With the loss of the stability of the Black female, Black children have since been on their own. The Black community has inadvertently given over its children to welfare, foster care, and an educational system that has no regard for the well being of the community. The Black community has now destroyed even the maternal family folk culture (though dysfunctional) that had sustained us throughout slavery and Jim Crow. The transference of stereotypical behaviors and mores have become the collective identity of Black America and it is having a destructive effect on a large percentage of the Black community. Frazier further wrote:

> Likewise, social and welfare agencies have been unable to stem the tide of family disorganization that has followed as a natural consequence of the

impact of modern civilization upon the folkways and mores of a simple peasant folk. Even Negro families with traditions of stable family life have not been unaffected by the social and economic forces in urban communities. Family traditions and social distinctions that had meaning and significance in the relatively simple and stable southern communities have lost their meaning in the new world of the modern city. (53)

The Black community still assumes racial stereotypes of the past for the chance to acquire the American dream. There has been a conscious decision to continually play the "nigger." You have the image of the good Negro, either folksy or urbane, who massages America's consciousness because he has embraced Americanism with no ill will of the past. On the other hand, you have the sullen Negro, the field Negro, and the hyper-sexual thug, bent on the destruction of the White American social structure. Both are exotic objects, and each consummates certain subconscious needs of the warped American psyche. One fulfills America's self image of benevolence, and the other provides (from a superior point of view) a physical outlet for White America to indulge its desire for violence and lust. The problem of the twenty-first century is no longer the color line, but to simply view ourselves as self aware human beings.

Matthew 16:26 For what is a man profited, if he shall gain the whole world, and lose his own soul? Or what shall a man give in exchange for his soul? (54)

THE ARRESTED DEVELOPMENT OF THE BLACK FEMALE

The Black woman is the foundation of the Black community. But that foundation was based in sexual degradation. Black women were not treated as women, but as instinctually sexual and fertile female beasts to be used for work and breeding. This abuse of the Black woman has left her with a damaged psyche that is evident even today and contributes to her present state of arrested development. Deborah Gray-White wrote:

> Since Black women were thought to be promiscuous, they could be raped, forced by their owners into illicit relationships with masters, overseers, and other slaves, and then be blamed for their own sexual exploitation. (1)

This degradation is most evident in the exploitation by White men in the form of rape/cross-breeding. This wholesale rape of Black females allowed for the legal perpetuation of slavery by automatically designating that the child be bound to the same condition as the mother. The Black American population has a high percentage of mulatto bastards as a consequence. The word mulatto is derived from the Spanish and Portuguese word mulato meaning young mule or hybrid. This wholesale rape intentionally followed accepted attitudes of animal husbandry that believed the offspring typically took the physical traits of the mother. Former slave Robert James wrote of the intentional cross breeding of Black women to White men to produce mulattos for the slave market. He wrote:

> From fifty to sixty head of women were kept constantly for breeding. No man was allowed to go there, save White men. From twenty to twenty-five children a year were bred on that plantation. As soon as they are ready for market, they are taken away and sold, as mules or other cattle. Many a man buys his own child. That is the cause of the rapid increase, already alluded to, of the mixed race. The Anglo-Saxon must blame himself for all the consequences that may result, in time or eternity, from such an unnatural state of things. I have seen brother and sister married together, and their children, some of them, as White as any person in the world. These children, marrying among the Whites, their children are White, and these have slaves, in their turn, after having been slaves themselves. On Wade Hamilton's farm the same process went on to a great extent, each planter vying with the other to see who could raise the greatest number of mulattoes a year for market, (as they bring a higher price than the Blacks,) the same as men strive to raise the most stock of any kind, cows, sheep, horses, (2)

The sexual relationship between White men and Black women until 1964 was a tradition of sex on demand. Until the enforcement of Civil Rights law, a White man could rape a Black woman at any time with impunity. A Black woman did not have the legal right to say no. These rapes were the physical nucleus of the Black American population. Rich Kittles, scientific director of African Ancestry, in Washington D.C., states that 30% of Black Americans who take DNA analysis to determine their African ancestry find that they are actually descended from a European male ancestor on their paternal side.(3) When a people are conquered, the men and women are enslaved. The conquerors take the women as spoils of war and by tradition rape them. This is done to break the paternal line of a people. When the paternal line of a people is physically broken by the victor; the former identity dies, and is replaced with one designated by the conqueror. It is a way to add insult to injury. It in a sense breaks the genetic link to Africa. In most societies, racial and cultural identities descend through paternal lines. We were no longer an African people, but Black American crossbreds with no name or history. We are the bastard sons and daughters of slaveholders and their mulatto sons. Former slave Mary Peters stated:

> My mother's mistress had three boys-one twenty-one, one nineteen, and one seventeen. One day, Old Mistress had gone away to spend the day. Mother always worked in the house; she didn't work on the farm, in Missouri. While she was alone, the boys came in and threw her down on the floor and tied her down so she couldn't struggle, and one after the other used her as long as they wanted, for the whole afternoon. Mother was sick when her mistress came home. When Old Mistress wanted to know what was the matter with her, she told her what the boys had done. She whipped them, and that's the way I came to be here. (4)

To break the paternal lines of a people is a form of paternal genocide. Currently Arab/Muslim raiders practice this technique in the Darfur region of Sudan. It intentionally creates an identity limbo, where the offspring can no longer bear the names of their forefathers, nor will the victor ever bestow his name or identity on bastard children out of the Black woman. Whites began to loosely apply the racial identity of "nigger" to describe this bastardized people called Black Americans. Slave Elias Thomas stated:

It took a smart nigger to know who his father was, in slavery time. I just can remember my mother. (5)

Paul Kalra's book, "From Slave To Untouchable Lincoln's Solution," contains a wealth of research about the sexual exploitation of Black women in slavery. Kalra's research states:

"A modern Southerner said 'the slave woman was to be had for the taking. Boys on and about the plantation inevitably learnt to use her, and having acquired the habit, often continued it into manhood or even after marriage ..." (6)

"Another Virginian affirmed that one of his slave women had all of her children 'by whoredom most of them gotten by White men' at a neighbor's house. For years, he wrote, these men had been sending for his slave women 'to whore it with' whenever he was away. Female slaves were quite accessible to both rural and urban non-slaveholders who desired casual sexual `` partners." (7)

This brutalization of the Black woman was so commonplace that it came to be accepted as a normal practice and some women began to feel no humiliation from being raped. Former slave Harriet Jacobs wrote:

> I know that some are too much brutalized by slavery to feel the humiliation of their position; but many slaves feel it most acutely and shrink from the memory of it. (8)

From the Harriet Jacobs quote, one can see that trauma programming can take such a strong root in the psyche of one that is oppressed, that he or she becomes physically, spiritually, and psychologically ambivalent to the dishonor and degradation enacted upon them. What Jacobs stated above supports Stanley Elkins comparisons of North American slavery to Nazi concentration camp torture and its behavior modification results. When one is subjected to and in this case born into traumatic circumstances, they adapt to that situation for physical preservation. In time, the degradation and dishonor can become normal, and one can begin to deduce a sense of pride from excelling within their lowly but clearly defined social role, this being the nigger wench.

Black Americans are many shades of brown. All of them are the result of this bastardization process. Light skinned Black Americans are a reflection of successive generations of bastardization. To many slave women, the increased mixture of White blood was considered an improvement, an honor over being a darker skinned woman. Slaveholders preferred mulatto slaves to pure Negroes. The lighter skinned quadroon and octoroons garnered the attention of White men. These lighter skinned women sought to raise their social standing through promiscuity, to further eradicate any semblance of African ancestry in their offspring.

This esteeming of White ancestry also shows up in John Howard Griffin's conversations with White males about miscegenation in his book, "Black Like Me."

> We figure we're doing you people a favor to get some White blood in your kids. (9)

Miscegenation in America was intended to be one-sided, White males to the Black females. Black women were a socially acceptable outlet for deviant behavior that could not be imposed upon White women. Stetson Kennedy recounts a Black minister who spoke out against miscegenation.

> A Negro minister who had from his pulpit deplored sexual relations between White men and Negro women was soon visited by a deputation of White businessmen who warned him to stop voicing such sentiments. (10)

Along with this degradation the slave woman was expected to increase her owners slave population, thereby increasing his assets. This was done with impromptu or with selective breeding arrangements. Animal husbandry rules of selective breeding were used on Blacks in the south. Blacks were regarded as valuable livestock and efforts to improve the hardiness and strength of the group increased profitability. Former slave Hilliard Yellerday stated:

> Master would sometimes go and get a large, hale, hearty Negro man from some other plantation to go to his Negro woman. He would ask the other master to let his man come over to his place to go to his slave girls. A slave girl was expected to have children from as soon as she became a woman. Some of them had children at the age of twelve and thirteen

years old. Negro men six feet tall went to some of these children. (11)

Harriet Jacob's statement also supports that forced and selective breeding of Black women did occur regularly:

> Women are considered of no value, unless they continually increase their owner's stock. They are put on par with animals. (12)

All Black women were expected to breed a baby every year, regardless of paternity. The goal was to produce good quality Negroes for sale at market. It closely follows a cattle or horse breeding operation where young offspring were sold after weaning from the mother. Slaveholders could not allow pair bonding, human decorum/family values, and paternity because those issues would conflict with the bottom line. Promiscuity at a young age was money in the pocket of slaveholders. Former slave John Smith states:

> My Master owned three plantations and three hundred slaves. He started wid two 'oman (women) slaves and raised three hundred slaves. One wuz called "Short Peggy," and the udder was called "Long Peggy." Long Peggy had twenty-five chilluns. Long Peggy, a Black 'oman, wusz boss of de plantation. Marster freed her atter she had twenty-five chilluns. Just thik o' dat-raisin' three hundred slaves wid two 'omans. It sho' is de trufe, do." (13)

A Black woman's worth was determined by her fertility and sexual performance. Some Black women drew honor from being a good breeder, a producer of many children, in which paternity did not matter. Former slave James Green states:

> More slaves was getttin' born dan dies. Old Moster would see to dat, himself. He breeds de niggers as quick as he can-like cattle- ' cause dat means money for him. He chooses de wife for every man on de place. No on had no say as to who he was goin' to get for a wife. All de weddin' ceremony we had was with Moster's finger pointin' out who was whose wife. If a woman weren't a good breeder, she had to do work with de men. But Moster tried to get rid of a woman who didn't have chillum. He could sell her and tell de man who bought he dat she was all right to own. But de nigger husbands weren't de only ones dat keeps up havin' chillum. De mosters and de drivers take all de niggers girls dey want. One slave had four chillum right after de other, with a White moster. Deir chillum was brown, but one of 'em was White as you is. Just de dame, dey was all slaves, and de nigger dat had chillum with de White men didn't get treated no better. She go no more away from work dan de rest of' em. (14)

The American south invented and maintained the nigger wench Black female identity for over two hundred years. The plantation system and later Jim Crow normalized the rape of Black women and illegitimate childbearing while denying them femininity, modesty, and respect. This trauma is evident today, as modern day Black women continue to sexually objectify themselves and exhibit hypersexual behavior in a twisted sense of pride. This sexual objectifying of self and the denial of feminine respect contributes directly to the arrested development of the Black female and to her present day personification of the Jezebel/Sapphire persona.

THE MODERN JEZEBEL/SAPPHIRE PERSONA

Some modern Black women have embraced two stereotypes; Jezebel or Sapphire. The Jezebel stereotype is the hypersexual Black woman. She is always looking for sex and readily available to men. Marilyn Yarbrough and Crystal Bennett wrote:

> Jezebel is depicted as erotically appealing and openly seductive. Her easy ways excused slave owners' abuse of their slaves and gave an explanation for Jezebel's mulatto offspring. This inability to be perceived as chaste brought about the stereotype of dishonesty. In other words, African American women were not, and often are not, portrayed as being truthful and, therefore, they could not be trusted. Throughout history, our court system has also exploited the myth of Jezebel. The courts have used this image to make racism and sexism appear natural. The sexual myth of Jezebel functions as a tool for controlling African American women. Consequently, sexual promiscuity is imputed to them even absent specific evidence of their individual sexual histories. This imputation ensures that their credibility is doubted when any issue of sexual exploitation is involved. (15)

Sapphire was the smart-mouth, domineering, and verbally aggressive woman. Sapphire is typified by the stereotypical combativeness in response to some offense or insult. Sapphire today would fit the Black woman who is always ready for a fight, crude, angry, and verbally abusive in her own right.

> In the stereotype of Sapphire, African American women are portrayed as evil, bitchy, stubborn and hateful. In other words, Sapphire is everything that Mammy is not. "The Sapphire image has no specific physical features other than the fact that her complexion is usually brown or dark brown." Unlike other images that symbolize African American women, Sapphire necessitates the presence of an African American male. The African American male and female are engaged in an ongoing verbal duel. Sapphire was created to battle the corrupt African American male whose "lack of integrity, and use of cunning and trickery provides her with an opportunity to emasculate him through her use of verbal put-downs." Ernestine Ward popularized the Sapphire image in the Amos and Andy television series. Ward played a character known as Sapphire, and her husband, Kingfish, was played by Tim Moore. Sapphire's spiteful personality was primarily used to create sympathy in viewers for Kingfish specifically and African American males in general. (16)

The modern Jezebel/Sapphire persona is a synthesis of the Sapphire and Jezebel stereotypes in which the Black woman is both combative and sexually loose. In a strange mix of racism, feminism, and tradition, the modern Jezebel/Sapphire persona has managed to merge two old stereotypes into one of the scantily clad, saucy, combative, ever sexually available whore of the inner city. Myth has become reality. To the Jezebel/Sapphire persona, sex is a biological need, not simply an urge. The biological needed is promoted in pornography and music videos. Young pre-teen girls now spend time developing dances that make their butt cheeks clap or wiggle at their discretion.

One only has to watch today's media outlets such as BET, MTV, and pornography to see the perpetuation of the Jezebel/Sapphire persona. The buttocks and thighs flapping on media outlets convey a base carnal nature that can only be satisfied by sexual degradation. The Jezebel/Sapphire persona takes pride in sexual acts that garner attention. The displays of dance seen on media outlets project a dark-hued female animal in heat. There is no honor among a people whose women flaunt their bodies in such ways. A woman's sexuality will always be a reflection of a peoples' collective identity. To be married, chaste, and self-controlled conveys a strong, family-centered culture, which Black America no longer has. Conduct determines respect.

The Jezebel/Sapphire persona allows women to be bred by as many men as she so chooses, via the rewards of feminism and the sexual revolution, but this also perpetuates the vestiges of slavery and Jim Crow. Unlike slavery, where the master chose a mate or bred the Black woman himself, feminism and the Jezebel/Sapphire persona have further dissolved paternal responsibility. This perpetuation of old stereotypes is manifested in blatant displays of sexuality by the modern day Black woman.

In 1994, a tape circulated around Washington, D.C. that depicted Black women stripping and masturbating to go-go music at a pool party in the metro area. The women were not coerced in any way.

In 1995, at Freaknic in Atlanta, Georgia, a young Black female walked into a crowd of Black males and flashed her breast. The men promptly touched and fondled her until a gentleman pulled her from the crowd, whom she chastised for helping her.

In 1995, at Daytona Beach Florida, a Black female driving a car on the strip proceeded to masturbate while in the driver's seat, inciting many men to jump on the car to watch the display. Police drove the men off.

The latest display of this blatant sexuality is in the Raleigh/Duke University rape case. DNA testing found genetic material from several males in the accuser's body and her underwear- but none from any Duke Lacrosse team members. (17) This false accusation, along with the DNA evidence of unnamed sex partners, simply reinforces the collective image of the innate sexuality of the Black woman.

Today the reference to a "baby daddy" is a community label which supports a historical racial stereotype. A "baby daddy" describes a man who has indiscriminately fathered a woman's child out of wedlock. It is simply a politically correct term for a stereotypical stud nigger.

This merging of feminism and racial tradition is devastating the Black family.

For the uneducated, working class Black woman, getting pregnant by a famous or high status man has financial incentives. Children born of such relationships are leverage, a financial asset to generate residual income from the labor of another. The author has spoken to women who seek to get pregnant by men of means and status, commonly professional Black athletes. If the child is a male, she also has the possibility of him having similar physical attributes, and thus, the same financial potential as his father. These ideas and motives draw upon the historic slave breeding program of the plantation south. Slaves were objectified physically for monetary gain through buying, selling, and breeding. The Black community has kept this tradition alive.

For the modern working Black women with an education, their own home, and independence, the Jezebel/Sapphire stereotype is also evident. A potential mate is now called a "maintenance man". The Black man's sole responsibility is to sexually fulfill or impregnate the Black woman at her discretion. But, a casual form of polygamy has evolved in which women now opt to share a man without the social or financial obligations that formal polygamous societies require. Women hope that over time the man may choose to form a monogamous relationship, or simply continue to provide them with occasional companionship.

There are now instances occurring where single women are opting for impregnation with the understanding that the father will have no emotional or financial role in the child's life, which mirrors slavery. The Jezebel/Sapphire persona accepts these casual polygamous relationships, but it's accepted because a long term relationship is not necessarily the goal. The goal is simply sexual gratification and casual procreation at her discretion via feminism. These relationships are usually casual and emotionally detached and often called a "booty call". This behavior closely aligns itself with the historic assumptions of Black sexual behavior.

Why is the Jezebel/Sapphire persona mentality so prevalent more than forty years after Civil Rights? Why have some modern Black women so fully embraced racial stereotypes? Author Shahrazad Ali wrote:

> The women in any civilization are indicative of the condition of the men. (18)

A people's honor is held by its women. The Black woman in America was not allowed any honor or virtue that would put her on equal footing with a White American woman. Sexual equality with White women was not, nor would it ever be allowed. Black women were, and still are, subconsciously considered flesh property to be used at its possessor's discretion for sexual gratification and financial gain.

To allow human attachment, family/pair bonding, and nuclear family structure would have allowed the humanity of such men and women to flourish, and would have condemned the institution of slavery. Subconsciously, Black women have continually embraced the mentality of the Jezebel/Sapphire persona down to the present day. There was always a segment of the community that lived in slave like oppression until the early 1960s, which enabled the generational transference of the habits and behaviors of women who have been repeatedly traumatized by rape, physical, and verbal abuse. The one aspect of the problem now which did not exist in the past is that the Jezebel/Sapphire persona is not condemned because Black women perpetuate this stereotype at their own discretion.

When a person internalizes that their physical presence or being is the sole cause of the sexual abuse inflicted upon them, they will either reject or embrace the label. Black women have been denied the opportunity to control their sexuality. In order to make some sense of this perpetual abuse, one may embrace the acts inflicted upon them as being fatalistic and become detached, a splitting of their personality to deal with trauma and to quell spiritual and psychological conflict. The acceptance of this label as readily available whores was always an under-current in the Black community. But the later interjection of feminism and the sexual revolution simply further chained Black women to their past under the illusion of freedom.

CARNAL INTUITION AND MALE ARCHETYPES

Nicolò Machiavelli wrote:

> "For my part I consider that it is better to be adventurous than cautious, because fortune is a woman, and if you wish to keep her under it is necessary to

beat and ill-use her; and it is seen that she allows herself to be mastered by the adventurous rather than by those who go to work more coldly. She is, therefore, always, woman-like, a lover of young men, because they are less cautious, more violent, and with more audacity command her." (19)

Machiavelli's comparison of women to fortune is evident in the choices that women make in men. It is a perfect description of basic sexuality among mammals. In the natural state, the male carries the urge to breed as many females as possible. Generally with men, it's quantity versus quality. The more progeny he produces, the better chance that his progeny survive to reproduce.

Females on the other hand, usually cannot produce more than one offspring at a time. In nature, females will submit to breeding by the strongest male available, the local Alpha male. The female is trying to increase her chances of producing healthy offspring by choosing the strongest male possible. The choice of breeding to the strongest male increases the probability of the offspring surviving to adulthood and to genetic perpetuation. Once she is bred, she is left to rear the offspring alone, or in a female herd group. In the Black community, this natural selection process described above is playing out. With lower marriage rates and high out of wedlock births, the Black community now resembles animalist patterns of breeding and courtship rather than normal human pair bonding and sexual relations.

Women will only half admit that they are attracted to aggressive, ill-tempered men out of a biological need. A recent study at the University of Michigan by Daniel Kruger found that the women viewed more masculine looking men as potential flings and less masculine looking men a long term partners. (20) In this study, the women were asked who they would choose for a short term relationship. The women said they associated traits such as risky behavior, violence, adultery, and bad parenting with masculinity, yet they still preferred men with these traits for short term relationships. (21)

Within the Black community, this ill-tempered, violent, detached man has become a collective archetype in the psyche of Black women. An archetype refers to a model from which all things of the same kind are copied or on which they are based; a model or first form; prototype. (22) The collective image of the "stud nigger," is fits the Jungian idea. This image is a collectively inherited unconscious idea, pattern of thought, image, etc., universally present in individual psyches. (23) This male archetype of Black women is now referred to as the brute or thug caricature based on the breeding Negro of the plantation.

In the Black community, gangsters, athletes, and entertainers are modern day breeding Negroes. They are perceived as aggressive, assertive, and prone to violence. They do this to maintain alpha male status and increase their opportunity for genetic perpetuation (sex). Most do not understand the nuances and responsibilities of manhood and fall back on carnal intuition to guide them in the sexual exploitation and abuse of women.

Black women when entertaining this archetype chase a myth, and not a flesh and blood man. The predominance of single parent households and exposure to males who perpetuate the breeding Negro archetype has set women up for bad decision making later in life. The lack of healthy male archetypes in early life leaves young women open to appropriating twisted images of manhood and womanhood. One common error among women lacking a protective father image is mistaking arrogance for strength. Many Black women as well as Black men do not have a true idea of manhood and masculinity. This lack of nurturing by a protective male archetype has resulted in self destructive behavior as a way to enhance a young woman's self-worth. The Motivational Educational Entertainment study found:

> A number of women said having multiple partners was the way to combat this devaluation. As for the chance to have lives of their own, these girls, the study's authors said, do not expect or "feel empowered" to achieve them. Since many do not expect exclusive relationships with partners, and sex is spoken of as a transactional relationship rather than an emotional one, keeping a partner by way of sex or pregnancy seems a viable strategy, at least temporarily. (24)

Among Black men and women, love and sex have dissolved into carnal posturing; men flaunting their prowess in business, sports, or whatever field they choose; women flaunting and gyrating their bodies to exhibit that they are in heat to attract the strongest male possible. Once copulation takes place, the male generally leaves and is ambivalent about any offspring he may have produced. Once pregnant, the female looks to her maternal-family support group of female friends and family to help rear the offspring. The child generally takes the name of the mother. In the Black community, this form of moral relativism makes promiscuity the norm today. It also makes paternity hard to determine, or irrelevant and reinforces the slave breeding pattern of unknown paternity, and the sexual availability of Black women. This behavior pattern is making the Black community more animalist, and less human with each generation. This generational pattern, reinforced with abusive or neglectful parenting, leaves women open to decision making based on a cycle of perpetual masochism.

MASOCHISM

Shahrazad Ali wrote:

> The Blackwoman does not know why certain kinds of pain and discord appeal to her. She doesn't know why she chooses misery over happiness. (25)

Why does the Black woman of today self sabotage? Why does the modern woman embrace the Jezebel/Sapphire persona mentality and enter into destructive relationships? Why do women yearn for stable productive men, yet sleep with immature, abusive males? Looking at history, it is all that the Black woman has known over the centuries in America. The reinforcing of low self-esteem through abuse has planted a masochist seed in successive generations of women. Masochism means the deriving of sexual gratification, or the tendency to derive sexual gratification, from being physically or emotionally abused. For the Black woman, it is a willingness or tendency to subject oneself to unpleasant or trying experiences. There is a high rate of sexual abuse of young women and girls. Many women who have been abused will often place themselves in drama-filled sexual situations where they act out their feelings about what happened to them [in the past].(26) Slavery in a sense laid the foundation of masochism, and Jim Crow carried it into the 20th century. It is another example of programming by trauma. The historical legacy of degradation and the current trend of promiscuity have lead Black women to value themselves as inanimate sexual objects and to take pleasure in such abuse. It reinforces the parameters of Blackness. Spiritually, the Jezebel/Sapphire persona mentality is akin to a generational curse. It is passed down from mother to daughter, father to daughter, brother to sister. It ties them to their past without a historical reference. All of the current behavior reflects generations of degradation that leads Black women to believe in their own mental and physical inferiority.

WHITE FEMINISIM

White women were expected to be chaste, modest virgins until marriage. When the feminist movement began, it promoted equal pay for equal work, professional fulfillment, and sexual freedom as a major goal. Society did not allow White women to be sexual outside of marriage. Feminism freed women sexually, but it also freed men from the social contract, the expectation that men were obligated to protect and provide for women in exchange for sex and/or love. The sexual revolution removed female leverage of sex in exchange for commitment and marriage. In the sexual revolution, White women wanted the opportunity to sleep with as many partners as they "chose". Black women fell headlong into this bad idea. Black women never had the choice of sexual partners. The goal of Black feminism would have been better served by demanding respect as women. Black women never received the nurturing or the pedestal of White womanhood. It was typical for Black women to work outside of the home, then come home and keep the house, and take care of children. Unlike the white upper income founders of the feminist movement, Black women often did not have the option of being housewives. Many of the feminist movement's founders were bored White women who wanted to fulfill their own egos rather than raise their children.

Black women having embraced the sexual revolution have only enhanced the image of the Jezebel/Sapphire persona of tradition. The sexual revolution simply enhanced an already negative image of Black women. Until Black women take control of their image, this pattern of behavior and racism will continue. Until Black women command the respect due mature, dignified women, nothing will change. People in the end are judged by their behavior. Black women cannot participate in acts that degrade their collective image, yet delude themselves that their actions and behavior do not affect the Black community.

THE PECOLA COMPLEX

Toni Morrison wrote:

> A little Black girl yearns for the blue eyes of a little White girl, and the horror at the heart of her yearning is exceeded only by the evil of fulfillment. (27)

Today you have Black women wearing blue and green contact lenses and blond hair extensions. It gives new meaning to Toni Morrison's "Bluest Eyes," the story of a poor Black girl so brutalized by her father and society that she yearns for blue eyes, the best known trait of the Aryan race. It would best be called, "The Pecola Complex." This inferiority complex runs so deep that Black women spend their time and money buying cosmetics to offset their Black skin. It's no different than the octoroon and quadroon slave women that wanted to eradicate/breed out any traits of Black ancestry. It's sad to watch modern Black women flaunting their newly purchased eyes and hair in the hopes of currying favor and respect from men. Such respect is not in the American tradition. The modern Black woman has no clear pattern of Black womanhood being respected and protected as have White women. White women were seen as the mothers of a superior people, and thus commanded respect. They were shunned if they slept around or seemed overtly sexual. Of the Black woman, such acts are said to be genetically inbred and unavoidable. The Pecola complex is the Black woman's envy of the social esteem reserved for

White womanhood. Sadly, in this quest for Whiteness, they do not realize that many White women cannot live up to the ideal. This quest to find equality with a myth also contributes to the arrested development of the Black female.

BIG MAMAS & MALE ARCHETYPES

> **Titus 2:3** The aged women likewise, that they be in behavior as becometh holiness, not false accusers, not given to much wine, teachers of good things; 4 That they may teach the young women to be sober, to love their husbands, to love their children, 5 To be discreet, chaste, keepers at home, good, obedient to their own husbands, that the word of God be not blasphemed. (28)

The Black community has a shortage of the female leadership needed to counter the mentality that now affects a significant percentage of the Black female population. The Black community no longer has its strong female matriarchs, commonly known as "Big Mamas." We now have male actors such as Martin Lawrence and Tyler Perry filling a void in the Black community through film versions of women who traditionally maintained the Black community. Big Mamas are dying out due mainly to the baby boomers wholesale rejection of Black culture. This new age, or 21st century grandmother, is of little use. These are women who refuse to embrace their age. The Black women of the baby boomer generation failed to look at the needs of younger Black women and provide the strength of character that their mothers demonstrated to hold families and communities together. They long for the strength and family cohesion of the traditional Black family, but do not want to do the work necessary to maintain family ties. Careers, middle class status, feminism, and outright selfishness are the essential causes of this loss of leadership. These women fail to realize that life is not really about them. It isn't about the job title, the McMansion, the model husband, the expensive weaves, and makeup. It's about the legacy you leave to your family. The baby boomer generation is leaving a legacy of emptiness. They have failed to pass on the coping/survival skills of previous generations and have hastened the demise of their own people in the process. The Black women of generation x, y, and z did not have the opportunity to receive or reject the lessons of their grandparents. Black women have more money at their disposal than at any other time in American history, but very little substance-other than the diva image which is essentially a cleaned up version of the Jezebel/Sapphire persona.

In order for this trend to be reversed, such women must realize that their time of sexuality is passed, and they must stop competing with their daughters and granddaughters for the attentions of men. They must accept that their best physical years are behind them, and it is now time for them to become emotionally available to younger women. These elder women (age 50 and over) of the Black community need to re-educate younger Black women about what it really means to be a Black woman, and that chastity and modesty are not passé. The older women of the community must lead by example, while also asserting more authority over younger women. They need to re-establish a female centered subculture within the Black community in which young Black women can be nurtured and guided. This calls for the establishment of a new matriarchal model, not born of the current feminist sexual empowerment movement. It must be one that complements a much needed new Black male patriarchal model. Currently, young Black women are simply following examples of the society at large, with patterns set by parents and grandparents of the sixties and seventies.

The replacement of the Jezebel/ Sapphire persona can only take place by a desire to change from within the Black female community. It must be initiated and lead by women, that Titus 2:3 calls "aged" women of the community, under a reconstructed matriarchal pattern that takes the best of the past and teaches it to the next generation.

The Black female must be given a new Black male archetype, and this begins with the father figure. Child sexual abuse, verbal abuse, and outright abandonment of females do have some bearing on decisions made in adult life. Sexual abuse along with the historical failure to nurture and protect Black women contributes to the current dilemma. This failure rests squarely on the shoulders of Black men. The consistent failure of Black men to play a daily and constructive role in the lives of their daughters reinforces the Black woman's inferiority complex. If Black men continue in this failure to nurture their daughters, nothing will improve. Daughters seem to naturally want their father's approval and attention. To deny a young girl this opportunity may hinder her in future relationships.

This also has to be taken into account with the internal archetype of Black women that contributes to this inferiority complex. Black women must consciously replace acquired archetypes of themselves and masculinity and make better choices in whom they date or with whom they maintain relationships.

ZERO TO NEGATIVE POPULATION GROWTH

The birth rate of Black America varies from zero to negative population growth. For a society to maintain zero population growth each couple must have 2.1 children, one to replace each parent. Typically, three children per couple allows for population growth and mortality. The American population has been in negative population growth since the

1960s, and immigration has been used to fill the void. Within the Black community, we have an interesting problem. As of 1992, 70% of Black women were unmarried. (29) We now have 67% of Black children born out of wedlock. (30) There is a trend in which if a single Black woman does have a child at all, it's only one child, which lends itself to negative population growth. The Black population is not replacing itself. The single mother with a large family is becoming uncommon. But whether or not we are in zero or negative population growth, single parent households are typically struggling financially and have a higher rate of juvenile delinquency.

- 45% of Black men have never married and 42% of Black women have never married.

- Married Black women declined from 62% to 31% between 1950 and 2002.

- By age 30, only 52% of Black women will marry compared to 81% of White women, 77% of Hispanics and Asians.

- Only 6% of Black men and 2% of Black women marry Whites.

- In 1970, just 33% of Black women, age 20-29 were unmarried. By 1992, that number exploded to 70%. (31)

According to the statistics, Black men and women are opting out of traditional marriages in exchange for living together or casual sexual relationships. The 2003 Virginia Office of Vital Statistics report states that 60% of all Black births in Virginia were to unmarried Black women.(32) Out of that, 38% of those unwed births were to Black women with a year or more of college education.(33) The report also found that Black women had the highest rates of abortion among all racial groups with a rate of 30.2 per 1000, double the rate of all other racial groups.(34) A 1977 Atlanta based study found that the birth rate among college educated Black women typically associated with the Black bourgeoisie is 1.5 children, which is negative population growth.(35) This lower fertility rate among educated Black women has been attributed to the difficulty of maintaining middle class status. This means that the upwardly mobile, educated segment of the population is on the decline, while the mass of the Black American population seems to be at zero population growth with 2.15 children per woman. (36) The low Black birthrates, of whom the majority are now out of wedlock births, points to a dying population. But among educated Black women the number of out of wedlock births is also increasing. According to the U.S. Census, only 30% of Black women marry. So if the other 70% of Black women do not marry, but have a child, that may correspond to the 67% out of wedlock birth rate of Black America. When you factor in the 1.5-2.15 birthrates, regardless of class or education, you have zero to negative population growth. On top of this, the rate of HIV infection among Black women is the highest of any racial group in the United States, comprising 67% of all heterosexual female HIV cases. (37) HIV primarily affects women in their prime reproductive years from ages 15-44, and is the third highest cause of death for Black women in the age group of 35-44. (38). Once the loss of current and future generations of Black women is felt, the family dynamic will be further stressed, leaving an already dysfunctional family structure worse off. When you lose women in their prime reproductive years, you lose your people. In the future, Black America may begin to mirror African HIV demographics with only the elderly and children left to maintain households. Debra Fraser-Howze,

President and CEO of the National Black Leadership Commission on AIDS states:

> What are we going to do when these women get sick? Most of these women don't even know they're HIV-positive. What are we going to do with these children? When women get sick, there is no one left to take care of the family. (39)

If the Black community's current trends continue as it appears they will, negative population growth will be felt. The predominance of female lead households and high out of wedlock births affects a community's ability to produce mature and responsible men and women. Adult Black men and women have introduced and reinforced a masochistic tendency among Black women that seems to have originated from paternal abandonment/absence or sexual abuse in childhood. Some women may feel that absent fathers do no love them and thus they devalue themselves via the Jezebel/ Sapphire persona. This paternally induced inadequacy leaves Black women open to exploitation in adult relationships by the over emphasis of sexual availability that directly contributes to high HIV infection rates. Black families are traditionally female centered, but we've now lost even that support system due to the shifting of priorities from family stability and the embracing of moral relativism.

THE ARRESTED DEVELOPMENT OF THE BLACK MALE

This scene took place on January 11, 2007 on the subway between the U.S. Capitol and the Dirksen building. The conversation took place between two Black women and one old White man. Of the two Black women, both were light skinned, one in her late thirties, the other in her mid-forties. The White man was a friendly doddering man of seventy or more years of age. The two Black women sat directly across from the old White man. The old White man continued his conversation with the younger Black women after they sat down on the train.

The old man said, "I feel like I've been on the road constantly for the past two months."

The Black woman replied, "Really, where have you been traveling?"

The old man said, "I've been all over for football games. I saw the quarterback from Kentucky. That kid was incredible. You should get your son to play, we could package him, and I could help you really get him out there."

The Black woman sat silently for a moment with a perturbed look on her face.

Then she blurted out, "MY SON IS A MORON! He can't decide what he wants to do. One week he wants to do this, the next he wants to do that. I'm sick of it. He doesn't get it from me. He gets it from his father and his family. They're all like that.

The old White man was silent. The comments of the White male and the Black female speak volumes about the perception of the Black male. Historically the Black male has been spiritually, emotionally, and financially emasculated by American society. The modern Black male is rarely thought of as a protector and provider. By tradition, the Black male has not been allowed to fully actualize manhood. This has caused conflict between Black women and Black men. Dr. Warren Farrell wrote:

> Those Black men with a slave heritage entered an industrialized era without adequate training to protect their families, they were rejected by women. Only the Black male performers-usually physical performers such as the Wilt Chamberlains and Magic Johnson-found thousands of women. Black men who could not perform were subject to ridicule in novels and films (e.g., The Color Purple, The Women of Brewster Place). As a result of this inadequate preparation to protect, many African-American men chose aberrant, quick fix, lottery-type attempts to "make it"- via drug dealing, gambling, or the lottery itself. (1)

One only has to look at Black men of the past to see the stifling of Black masculinity in society. Gabriel Prosser, Nat Turner, Denmark Vesey, Marcus Garvey, Malcolm X, and Martin Luther King Jr. all died asserting their right to freedom and fully actualized manhood. Most of these men understood that the desire to live free would require their physical deaths. These men died rebelling against a system that today is still intimidated by Black manhood.

By tradition, Black women understood that Black men had no power to provide for, protect, or avenge their sexuality. If a White man raped a Black woman and a Black male family member retaliated against the White perpetrator, he would be killed as an example of White supremacy. This instilled the fear of death. The fear of losing a loved one caused many women to compromise the honoring of their sexuality. Rather than lose a husband or family member, Black women would not tell their loved ones of sexual assaults and insults. Harriet Jacobs wrote in "Life of a Slave Girl" about an incident where her master insulted her in front of her brother, William. Harriet was sexually harassed daily by her master to become his concubine. Jacobs wrote:

> I felt humiliated that my brother should stand by, and listen to such language as would be addressed only to a slave. Poor boy! He was powerless to defend me; but I saw the tears, which he vainly strove to keep back. (2)

Jacobs states her humiliation in her brother's inability to act on her behalf. She loved her brother deeply, but her respect was lost in this act of emasculation by his master. This feeling, a mix of anger/humiliation at the impotence of Black masculinity, is the crux of Black male and female relationships today. Her brother's inaction in asserting his masculinity fits perfectly within the parameters of Blackness set by the Black codes and Jim Crow. Mothers and sisters rather than physically lose their loved ones, neutered Black males. They have learned consciously or unconsciously that sexual abuse upon their mothers and sisters is normal, and that their sexual honor should not be defended. Black women became the protective buffer between White men and Black men. This physical "protection" of Black men by Black women is a role reversal and it emasculates the male. The cost to women was their sexuality. The cost to Black men was self respect. Harriet Jacob's incident was one in which she and her brother both learned to live with shame. Black women made an unconscious social compact to keep their sons alive as perpetual boys in exchange for their sexuality. This learned mechanism of living with shame makes a man hollow. In this pattern, Black women have subconsciously learned that Black males are not men, and should always be protected by Black women from White Society.

The shame and denial of Black masculinity is a learned survival mechanism that emasculates men psychologically, spiritually, and economically, leaving them open to reap contempt from White society and mockery within Black America. This tradition of emasculation is the root cause of the arrested development of the Black male. E. Franklin Frazier's work dealt with this issue, where he wrote specifically about the Black middle class:

> As one of the results of not being able to play the "masculine role," middle-class Negro males have tended to cultivate their "personalities" which enable them to exercise considerable influence among Whites and achieve distinction in the Negro world. Among Negroes they have been noted for their glamour. In this respect they resemble women who use their "personalities" to compensate for their inferior status in relation to men. This fact would seem to support the observation of an American sociologist that the Negro was "the lady among the races," if he had restricted his observation to middle class males among American Negroes. (3)

This feminization process was necessary for the middle class Black man to exist. The effeminate or passive personality traits that Frazier talks about are still evident today. In the present day, it is obvious that many Black males down play the masculine role to make themselves more palatable to White America. In the past, economic opportunities were limited to menial jobs with no upward mobility. Nor could a Black male operate any kind of business if Whites felt he equated his masculinity with that of White men. Such Black men were beaten, killed, or marginalized within their community by social contract. E. Franklin Frazier wrote:

> "In the South the middle-class Negro male is not only prevented from playing a masculine role, but generally he must let Negro women assume leadership in any show of militancy. This reacts upon his status in the home where the tradition of female dominance, which is widely established among Negros, has tended to assign a subordinate role to the male" (4)

Many a Black household gathered around the grandmother or mother as the spiritual leader and protector of a family. It's a tradition born out of necessity, but it has left a void of Black male leadership in many households. Typically, such families may have a silent paternal man who caters to the desires of his Sapphire type wife. Many of these men withdrew into womanizing and drug or alcohol abuse to fill the void of lost manhood. Like Harriet Jacob's brother, William, these men learned to live with shame. These men feared the retribution of White society if they asserted themselves and preceived failure in the eyes of their wives and daughters if they did not provide for, protect, and successfully lead a family.

In lower class households, the tradition of racism kept many Black men from being financially able to provide for a family. In 1963, Thomas Pettigrew wrote:

> Employment discrimination has traditionally made it more difficult for the poorly-educated Negro male to secure steady employment than the poorly-educated Negro female. In many areas of the nation, North as well as South, this is still true, with Negro females always able to obtain jobs as domestics if nothing else is available. When the unskilled Negro male does manage to secure a job, he generally assumes an occupation that pays barely enough to support himself-much less a family. Such conditions obviously limit the ability of lower-class Negroes to follow the typical American pattern-that is, a stable unit with the husband providing a steady income for his family. The Negro wife in this situation can easily become disgusted with her financially-dependent husband, and her rejection of him further alienates the male from family life. Embittered by their experiences with men, many Negro mothers often act to perpetuate the mother-centered pattern by taking a greater interest in their daughters than their sons. For example, more Negro females graduate from college than Negro males, the reverse of the pattern is found among White Americans. (5)

A little over forty years later, the gulf between Black men and women has grown. This growing education and income gap is creating a gender based class system within the Black community. Women tend to marry at their socio-economic level or above it. With this shortage of educated professional Black men, the Black middle class cannot replace itself. This income and education disparity is the bane of many Black women who essentially do not want to marry or date "down." Black women are angered by this pattern of the under-educated/under-employed Black man, but it's the norm of the Black community, and has been for generations. Many Black men have no idea what it means to be a "man," much less a father or husband. But this problem stems partly from the increase in female lead households. In 1965, Dr. Carroll Quigley wrote about the United States Middle Class Crisis in his book, "Tragedy and Hope". He discussed the modern middle class family and the weakening of the family structure. He noted that in female centered families, young women were demonstrating more advanced preferences and behaviors due to the mother's parental steering. Quigley wrote:

> Emotional readiness to face the fact of one's sexuality comes earlier and earlier for the girls today, but later and later for the boy, chiefly because the middle-class mother forces independence and recognition of the fact that she is a woman upon her daughter, but forces dependence and blindness to the fact that he is a man upon her son. (6)

Within the Black community this assertion rings true for those in the middle and low class. There is a saying in the Black community, that Black women raise their daughters and baby their sons. This effect came about due to the suppression of Black masculinity. In order to preserve the life of her male child, she contributed to the arrested development of the Black male. Black women have unconsciously taught their sons to live with shame, to not be men. These women understood that their sons had to accept the social order of their day to live. Those that rebelled against the social order were generally tortured and killed. Malcolm X noted that his father and at least three of his uncles died violent deaths because they rebelled against the social order.

In the Black community, with its predominately female run households, Black males are being raised to be dependent upon women and have become very irresponsible as a consequence. It is so ingrained, that there is now no shame in dependence upon a female. This lack of shame manifests itself in an extended adolescence that hinders the emotional development of the Black male. Without a male or a female that makes a boy accountable for his actions and forces awareness of his manhood and its responsibilities, he will essentially remain in a childlike state. It is not far fetched to assert that modern Black females are subconsciously contributing to the problem of Black male dependence and passivity.

Quigley's assertion of female marital frustration within the White middle class family manifests itself in a strangely similar pattern in the Black community. Quigley asserts that the middle class wife's insecurity in her relationship with her husband forces her to compete with her daughter for her husband's attention, but too also smother and over protect the son so as to keep him emotionally dependent upon her. (7) She is making her son a substitute companion or husband. Taken a step further into the Black community, we see many Black females frustrated with the Black male's inability to commit, provide, and protect.

Many divorced and single mothers may have some anxiety or anger over failed relationships that they could not control. A male child may provide the mother with the opportunity to keep a male counterpart in her life. This need for a surrogate male may cause many mothers to coddle and befriend their sons, while pushing their daughters into intellectual pursuits and educational opportunities. Many children are socially drawn to the parent of opposite gender in childhood. But in the end the male influence or the lack of a male influence upon young Black males seems to play a larger factor in Black masculinity. The November 19, 2006 edition of the Washington Post series "Being a Black Man," published an article entitled "The Meaning of Work." The Black male subject of the article struggled with finding employment. The subject's friend, Mike Rogers, sums up the problem:

> He described the men who lived in the building as "bums. Total drunks. In and out of jobs." The women, he said, were women who "settled for less," and as for the children: "We did more adult things at extremely young ages than anybody that I knew. It was just so much going on, and we were always around adults, but it was a constant party for them. All they did was drink, they tried to drink themselves out of their misery, or smoke themselves out of their misery. So we always saw all the adult things. Everything was always right in front of us."

Mike goes on to say:

> The bottom line is you are having to learn what some man -- your dad, or somebody -- should have been instilling in you as a child. We didn't get that. We lacked the male influence. That's why you run around here, you can't make up your mind." (8)

When the older male influences within a community are bad or nonexistent, you have grown men who have no idea what it means to be a man. Manhood comes down to accepting personal responsibility for all of your actions or decisions. But the trend of female lead households has crossed over into the Black educated middle class population, so the problem cannot be totally laid at the feet of the Black masses. The problem is that Black males are not being groomed to be men, then husbands, and fathers. It seems that people simply hope that the male will figure out for himself how to model himself into a responsible man. In the end, the males are indecisive, passive, and ambivalent about education, manhood, and fatherhood because they have no visual foundation from which to draw. In a December 17, 2006 article of the Washington Post, "Dad, Redefined," Tony Dugger, a fatherhood activist, states:

> Guys are doing what they learned at home. They care about their kids emotionally, but they don't see it as odd that they don't live with them. You can't tell them they're doing something wrong because their life experience tells them it's normal. (9)

The ambivalence towards women in adult relationships also stems from mothers exposing young boys to an endless succession of useless male suitors. Young boys have an innate desire to please and protect their mothers. If the mother appears promiscuous or tolerates abusive relationships, young boys lose respect for their mothers. Generations of Black men have been raised in this pattern of exposure to the promiscuous lifestyle of the mother, yet are financially and emotionally dependent upon her. In such a situation, manhood is difficult to achieve. It is a replay of the Jacobs episode in which William could not defend his sister's honor. Today this is reflected in the son's inability to defend the mother against unacceptable male attention. But in modern times, the Black female is complicit in this abuse, unlike previous generations. This may cause boys to then develop an ambivalent attitude toward sex and male responsibility. Many a woman states that she feels she's married a child because of his dependence or passivity. A good number of Black men feel no remorse at a woman pulling all of the financial and emotional weight in their relationships. Many modern Black women feel that they may need to mother their mate, to develop the men they are dating, by doing homework in college, paying for meals and trips, footing the mortgage, rearing the children, and providing sexual intimacy. There seems to be significant amount of gender role confusion in Black relationships. Thomas Pettigrew found confusion in sex role adoption in homes with single parent households. Pettigrew wrote:

> Mothers raising their children in homes without fathers are frequently overprotective, sometimes even smothering in the compensatory attempts to be a combined father and mother. (10)

For Black males who choose to express their masculinity without an archetype, the streets give them an avenue. In our current predicament, 70% of Black children are born out of wedlock, meaning the father is available only part-time or completely out of the picture. The developing Black male is left in a precarious situation because he has no external motivation, no father figure to aid in becoming independent. Quigley writes about the middle-class boy who must free himself of dependence on his mother by his own inclination:

> The position of the middle-class boy becomes more complex and pitiful, since he not only must face the fluctuating chronology of these developments to a greater degree but must free himself from his emotional dependence on his mother with little help from anyone. (11)

The desire of a male to free himself from motherly dependence has become more pronounced in the Black community because young Black males are left to build their idea of Black masculinity from the men around them such as womanizers, drunks, drug dealers, and pimps.

THE STUD NIGGER PERSONA & MISOGYNY

In the absence of a respected place within a society, people will create their own society. The formation of street culture is a direct result of estrangement from the American mainstream and from the Black community. Few Black males head families, marry, or take leadership positions in their communities. The Black community as a whole is female headed. Even the Black middle class male sees little masculinity in the bourgeoisie Black male image. As a result, they have begun to emulate the thug/brute persona to develop and express their masculinity.

This has resulted in the thug mentality. The thug mentality has its origins in the mythic "stud nigger" of the old south. The bad nigger was an oversexed, physically strong Black man of limited emotional and intellectual ability which many Black males now aspire to emulate. Former Slave Lewis Jones spoke about the breeding nigger:

> My mammy am owned by Massa Fred Tate and so am my pappy and all my brudders and sisters. How many brudders and sisters? Lawd A'mighty! I tell you, cause you asks, and dis nigger gives de facts as 'tis. Let's see; I can't 'lect de number. My pappy have twelve chillum by my mammy and twelve by anudder nigger, name' Mary. You keep de count. Den, dere am Lisa. Him have ten by her. And dere am Mandy. Him have eight by her. And dere am Betty. Him have six by her. Now, let me 'lect some

more. I can't bring de names to mind, but dere am two or three others what was jus' one or two chillum by my pappy. Dat am right-close to fifty chillum, ' cause my mammy told me. It's disaway; my pappy am de breedin' nigger. (12)

Currently, the Black community quietly accepts this idea of manhood without responsibility. Black masculinity is relegated to athleticism, sexual prowess, and violent behavior. The thug/athlete identity is the pre-dominate way modern Black men and women relate to each other.

The Black male population interacts with itself and the larger community through the stud nigger image. Discussions of politics, culture, or any intellectual pursuits will get you ostracized. The main reason so few Black males take up intellectual pursuits is because it is not equated with Black manhood. The idea of being "down" is a reflection of that. The main reason the Black bourgeoisie has so few eligible heterosexual Black males is because the image of an intellectual Black male is not accepted by the Black community. He would have to have a sports background or a reputation as a womanizer to be accepted. This also reflects why we produce so few engineers, inventors, and intellectuals in various fields. The Black man is about 150 years behind in his thinking. Black manhood is based on the southern idea of "honor" but is now referred to as respect in the Black community. In Fox Butterfield's book, "All God's Children The Bosket Family and the American Tradition of Violence," he wrote:

Above all, honor meant reputation; a man's worth resided in the opinion of others. Honor also meant valor, a man had to be prepared to fight to defend his honor if challenged or insulted. (13)

White manhood entailed representing his family name and also defending his reputation. The dictionary defines honor as honesty, fairness, or integrity in one's beliefs and actions. This idea of honor was never extended to Black men or women. With the Black males' inability to provide, protect, and to receive fair and honest treatment from society at large, a smaller more criminal version of honor sprung up called "RESPECT." Without the respect of your peers you are nothing. Physical brawn and the inclination to use violence is what received respect in the Black community. Black males had to demonstrate that they would not be servile to the White inhabitants of the south. Those that demonstrated the ability to intimidate Whites by action and reputation were highly esteemed in the southern community, but it left Black males with a one dimensional identity.

White awe at innate Black male athletic prowess creates an almost supernatural image. Athletics are one area that Black males have been allowed to dominate. In a Yahoo Sports Article, "Downside to Athleticism," a White NFL player, Wayne Gandy, talks about the assumed athleticism of the Black quarterback. Gandy states:

> When fans and coaches see a Black quarterback, it's automatic that they expect to see a guy who is more athletic," Gandy said. "So what happens when you get around the goal line or you get in those situations where most quarterbacks are taught to throw it away or get rid of the ball for a short gain if the play breaks down? The Black quarterback is told, "Do something, make a big play." (14)

Black males now have the highest rate of incarceration due to aspiring to live up to an identity born of racism. This is an aspect of the arrested development of the Black male, the belief in the inferiority of one's self and the belief in the historically designed parameters of Blackness. In fulfilling one of the two roles accepted in playing the nigger, Black males are saying, "If I'm a nigger, I'm going to be the baddest nigger around."

Along with this negative self image held by Black men, many Black women believe it also. Many Black women honestly believe that Black men lack the capacity to operate in environments that require abstract thought. Nor does the Black community intellectually track its Black males. It's believed that Black males only make it to success through sports or music. The Black community has not equated superior intellectual ability as something worthy of respect. It is usually something that is mocked or laughed at.

This leaves Black males with two paths; that of the athlete or the thug. Both of which are impotent in regards to the Black community or mainstream America with one exception, the stud nigger persona. The stud nigger persona espouses the superiority of Black men as lovers. It's the converse of the female Jezebel/Sapphire persona. The stud nigger persona is another assumed stereotype held by White America with a sense of fascination. John Griffin in "Black Like Me," quotes White ideas of Black male sexuality. He wrote:

> He asked about the size of Negro genitalia and the details of Negro Sex life. Only the language differed from the previous inquirers – the substance was the same. The difference was that I could disagree with him without risking a flood of abuse or petulance. He quoted Kinsey and others. It became apparent he was one of those young men who possess an impressive story of facts, but no truths. This again would have no significance and would be unworthy of note except for one thing: I have talked to such men many times as a White and they

never show the glow of prurience he revealed. The significance lay in the fact that my Blackness and his concepts of what my Blackness implied allowed him to expose himself in this manner. He saw the Negro as a different species. He saw me as something akin to an animal, in that he felt no need to maintain his sense of human dignity, though certainly would have denied this. (15)

Griffin's observations prove that the stud nigger persona is a White supremacist construct. The Black community's complicity in fulfilling this role is another example of false consciousness. Promiscuity is also essential in the perpetuation of this identity. The stud nigger persona is misogynist by nature in that it creates an atmosphere of emotional abuse of women who are making decisions generally based on pair bonding. Many Black males take pride in objectifying themselves in sex or sports for some sense of self-esteem which falls within the parameters of Blackness. In America, there are now groups of Black men who provide swinger fantasies for white couples who want to experience the stereotypes in a safe and clean environment. Art Hammer, the Mandingo party coordinator, said:

"The fantasy goes both ways. The women get to fuck our guys while their husbands watch, and we get to fuck rich white women, really mutt 'em out. It works! But people in this lifestyle are affluent-I'm talking judges, CEOs, FBI agents, important people-so before they invite a bunch of black men to their homes, they want to know they're safe, they're not going to get robbed, and everyone is discreet. So that's what I provide-a gentlemen in the street and a thug in the bedroom."(16)

These Black men are playing both the good nigger and the bad nigger. Most of Art Hammer's stable of Mandingos have college degrees and hold professional jobs. They have made a conscious choice to fulfill the traditional stereotype of the stud nigger while also providing white couples with peace of mind that they are also safe as they indulge racist fantasies. Why have they made this choice? Why are they willing to interact with white people according to white assumptions of Blackness? It is because they still suffer from a black inferiority complex, and only derive self-esteem by fulfilling traditional roles constructed by White America. They have no identity of their own. The sexual prowess of Black males is a source of pride. Engaging in promiscuity and producing illegitimate children is equated with Black manhood.

With the younger generation of Black men, there is now a deep hatred of women. A study conducted by Motivational Educational Entertainment (MEE), noted this shift within the Black community.

> The most telling attitudinal change from the "movement" years is the absence of any influence of feminism and the open disdain for Black women. (17)

All of the children surveyed for the (MEE) were born after 1980. They are the children of the first Hip-Hop Generation or Generation X, people born between 1965-1980. The belief that Black women are to be used and exploited is common. In this street society, weakness of any kind will not be tolerated. In a predatory culture, opportunities to prey upon weakness are exploited. In nature, predators/scavengers look for weakness, an easy target to feed upon. It is no different in street culture. Women, children, and families are targets of opportunity. Black men have now formed a closed society based on animalistic traits. If someone appears physically weak, young or old, they are a target of opportunity. Rosa Parks' mugging by Black youths is a demonstration of this mentality.

Within Black male groups, the competition for Alpha male status is intense. From playing the dozens, to slap boxing, to rapping, it's all an opportunity to display bravado and detachment from emotion. To show any emotion other than anger is weakness. Respect is based on the idea that one will do harm to you if you attempt to make them a target of opportunity.

This emotional detachment and the reliance on violence is another aspect of the arrested development of the Black male. Oftentimes, abusive relationships are ones in which men have not learned to deal with their emotions in any other way than physical outbursts that reflect a child's tantrum. This mentality is developed as a survival mechanism in dysfunctional and hostile environments. To keep the other predators at bay, one must appear a predator.

This thug/brute persona and its role requirements also contribute to the rift between Black men and women. If further widens the education and income gaps between Black women and Black men. We are coming to a point where Black men are really not necessary in the modern world. Warren Farrell wrote:

> For different reasons, few Whites or Blacks are willing even to discuss how the use of the Black male as a field slave required a greater dependency on physical strength for most Black men than it did for Black women-and that it is physical strength that current technology makes increasingly irrelevant. (18)

This marginalized manhood has been prevalent through American history and usually expresses itself in self destructive behaviors and violence toward others. The tradition of the south was to use violence as a means of control via whipping and lynching. When you suppress a man's masculinity it will manifest itself in other ways, and in some Black American families, violence toward women was the outlet. Control of Black women through violence allowed Black males to express their suppressed masculinity against individuals who held a lower rung in society than themselves.

This thug/brute persona is a copy of the stereotypical strong southern White male image that demanded absolute respect and obedience and was referred to as the "man." Black men simply brought into the home how they were treated in public. In such cases, when a wife or girlfriend insults or disobeys a Black man, she dishonors him, and he must confront her insult or disobedience with violence to maintain his honor. In most societies if you cannot control your woman, you are not a man. This behavior has set the masses on a course that has caused the masochism of the Black female. Much of Black American literature reflects this thug/brute character that migrated with the masses from the rural south to the northern urban environment. The thug/brute persona is an archetype in the consciousness of Black America. It makes the exploitation and abuse of Black women by Black men normal.

At the same time many, Black women have ventured into professional and intellectual endeavors in which Black men lag behind. This makes the Black man and his reliance on physicality more pathetic, and increases his dependence on females for survival.

This dependence upon females, be it mother, spouse, or friend, also manifests itself in the pimp and player mindset prevalent in today's Black community. Some Black men now see a woman as a financial means to an end. Black men have spun dependence upon a woman into a commodity that he controls, called pimping.

The idea of pimping women is steeped in terminology meant to turn a woman into an animal. Terms and phrases such as: turned out, on the track, stable, bitch or bitches are all animal terminology used on women who are marketed by men as prostitutes. The term "turned out" originated in the equestrian community to mean that the horse is well presented for competition. The track is the race course of competition which now means the segment of the street where prostitutes congregate. A stable is actually a barn for horses, but in pimping it refers to the pimp's inventory of women under his care and guidance. The term bitch means female dog, but when used on women it can mean an irritable women or a woman who demonstrates dog-like submission to her pimp. It is meant to dehumanize a woman. Pimping entails finding out what a woman's desire or weakness is, then exploiting it by promising to fulfill that void in exchange for total control of her person. The pimp is giving the woman an opportunity to earn his love and attention by making him money through prostitution. These women are providers for men. These women tend to have a need for male companionship that is based in masochism. This generally arises among women that have been neglected, abused, or abandoned by men in their early lives. They have had either a bad archetype or no archetype. A pimp becomes the male archetype these women feel they need. In exchange, the women prostitute themselves to support this surrogate father or husband. These women have little self worth, and to receive some semblance of male attention from their perceived archetype in being a prostitute or a bitch in his stable is the essence of pimping. This is a transactional relationship in which if the woman gets out of line, he denies his presence to the woman. These women feel they are nothing without the attention and reputation of their pimp to represent them. The relationship may be violent at times, but these women are so damaged that to some, violence is actually a form of positive attention.

This pimp ideal also shows up in the mainstream Black community. It is present in the mother son relationship in which the mother is financially supporting the son in adulthood. This pimp ideal also shows up in many Black male/female relationships in which the female or females financially support the Black male they are involved with. If the female, be it mother or spouse, puts too much pressure on the Black male he leaves, thereby denying the woman his presence, or he reacts violently. These men are exploiting their mothers' and spouses' fear of being alone. This fear of being alone has allowed many men to engage in casual polygamy which is very similar to the pimp dynamic. The men receive financial support from the women in exchange for male companionship. In this gender role reversal, women finance the illusion of a protective male companion. In actuality, the male has no power other than his presence and image.

We now have Black males who take pride in the "spreading my seed," trend which falls under the "baby daddy" label. This is where Black males impregnate as many females as possible. The Black male is again fulfilling the traditional role of the stud nigger. History has restricted Black males from social and economic opportunity. Sexual potency and the ability to catch and impregnate females without the financial responsibilities or social obligations has been a source of pride since slavery. It seems that with the degradation of the Black women by White men, Black men have followed suit, further degrading Black women through the indiscriminate fathering of offspring, physical abuse, and abandonment. But in our modern world, under the definition of feminism, such men are generally absolved of any wrong doing. Under strict feminism, men are no longer obliged to provide, protect, or sacrifice for a woman's needs or happiness. This male is called the feminist male.

THE FEMINIST MALE

This modern Black male would best be described as the forerunner of the "Feminist Male." Present day America plays up the "Metrosexual" man, but the feminist male would be a better term for the modern man of America. With the rise of the feminist movement, White America is now beginning to see social trends that look quite similar to traditional Black families. Men, Black or White, are no longer seen as providers, protectors, or leaders. Roughly three generations of men have been reared in households where both parents work. Women have the right to pursue career, hobbies, then family if they so choose. With these gains, they must understand that men have accepted women as being financially independent individuals that must pull their own weight. This is the feminist backlash, where many men will not financially support a woman's desire to fulfill the traditional role of mother and wife. Men are no longer under any social pressures to marry or have children, or to get married if they have children out of wedlock. Men no longer tolerate the traditions of chivalry, courtship, nuclear family, and the responsibility of being the sole bread winner. Feminist men have no qualms with single parenting, cohabitating, or staying single. Feminism has allowed men to concentrate on themselves. Life for the feminist man is no longer about self-sacrifice, marriage, children, and a mortgage. They make use of their time in promiscuous sex or hobbies. A woman's happiness, personal fulfillment, family aspirations, and financial security are her responsibility.

This is the main reason, the best selling book "The Rules," no longer works in relationships. Men don't abide by tradition in courtship and marriage, yet many women still seek these traditions. Women have removed the feminine aspects of being a women. Feminism and the sexual revolution threw away the sexual leverage of their grandmothers. Feminist men are now voting with their feet and you see lower marriage rates and higher divorce rates as a result. Dr. Warren Farrell wrote:

> Men became more passive-aggressive. Men increasingly felt that their only relationship power was not getting into one. Women labeled this a fear of commitment, accused men of a fear of intimacy, and began making masculinity virtually synonymous with evil. (19)

Today, 50% of marriages end in divorce, birthrates are declining, and more men choose to live with a woman, or not marry at all. This is because the modern marriage is not empowering to men, nor does it fit the masculine gender role that men seek to fulfill. The modern marriage in America is a mirror image of the gender role shift that took place within the Black community due to slavery and Jim Crow. Many marriages today are beginning to look like long term homosexual (domestic partnership) arrangements rather than a traditional marriage. But in the modern marriage, economic empowerment was the catalyst.

Now the majority of Black males are not raised under traditional gender roles that foster nuclear families. Without a traditional male role to emulate, young men create their own idea of masculinity. When young men are left to their own devices and ideas of manhood you get men who are masculine in appearance, but still dependent upon women for daily survival. Such men now take pride in being a "pimp" a man that lives off of women even if it's his mother. When you factor in ambivalence toward the females, and the desire to turn dependence upon woman into a masculine image, you have a feminist male. With the assuming of a contrived form of manhood through misogyny, gang culture, and violence as a means to express Black American manhood, you have the feminist male. These males are simply misguided boys in every sense of the word.

BLACK MALE SEXUAL IDENTITY AND HOMOSEXUALITY

There have been some studies that link Black male sex role confusion to excessive violence and promiscuity. Hyper-sexuality may be a form of overcompensation for this sexual identity confusion. The bravado, a propensity toward violence, and the loud overbearing bully types seem to need to "front" to cover up some emotional need or weakness in their life. Thomas Pettigrew found that males from single parent or female lead households require that they achieve a masculine self image later in their childhood after having established an original self-image on the basis of the only parental model they have had-their mother. (20) Pettigrew goes on to refer to a study entitled, "Children of Bondage" which reported the problems that arise from an absent or weak father image. The study noted that in matrifocal families girls tended to setup similar female lead households and that the boys were found to have a sexual identity conflict that was compensated for by gang culture and acting out through excessive violence along with the total rejection of femininity in every form be it women or effeminate men. (21) Pettigrew's conclusion supports the finding of the Motivational Educational Entertainment Survey which found young Black males have developed a hatred or aversion to Black women and any form of feminism.

Again it brings the argument back to the need to express masculinity through sex and violence. Currently in the Black community, bisexuality and homosexuality are problems the Black community cannot afford. Already emasculated by society, the men hide their sexual identity problems while perpetuating a masculine persona. In the Black community, gender roles have been interchangeable. Masculine and feminine behaviors are flexible within the Black community. This fluidity of gender roles also shows up in the prison culture in which Black prisoners rape White prisoners. It is essentially a tit for tat deal for the emasculation many Black males feel outside of prison. A prison rape victim reported:

> Why prison sexual assault occurs: Part of it is revenge against what the non-White prisoners call, "The White Man," meaning authority and the justice system. A common comment is, "ya'll may run it out there, but this is our world!" More of it I think is the assaulters own insecurities and them trying to gain some respect in their peer group by showing that they "are a man." This subculture is concerned with appearances, and the more imposing an appearance, the more respect you command. Some of the guys I rode with didn't want any sex or $. They just wanted the status of having a "Kid." Naturally, I liked them best. — S.H., Texas, 9/10/96 (22)

This need to establish dominance over another man or to be submissive to another man may have some basis in sexual identity confusion. This goal of emasculating other men, to break any connection they may have with masculinity, does have its origins in the southern tradition of emasculating Black males. It's a way to shame a male with something he must live with for the rest of his life. To brand a man with shame is worse than killing him outright, because it destroys his identity and self-esteem as a man. The phrase "making him my bitch" best describes taking a male's manhood as a way to destroy his identity as a man. Prison rape leaves men with two options, retaliate or submit. If he retaliates he will probably be injured, maybe killed. If he submits, he gives his manhood over to the aggressor, and in prison society, he is forever a bitch. This prison test parallels the southern tradition of Black men who either submitted to their place or rebelled against the system. By tradition, White males would kill a Black man that looked them in the eye or stood up for himself. To combat this, many Black males were taught to live with shame, to accept insults and humiliation. The bad Negro will not live with shame, his honor (respect) compels him to retaliate or he will forever be the White man's "bitch".

In J. L. King's Book, "On The Down Low," the author describes the sex role dynamics of homosexual affairs.

> A bottom is the "passive," or receptive, partner in anal sex. Some men refer to themselves as "total bottoms," because they prefer receptive sex only;" (23)

He goes on to explain that:

> "Most men are socialized to accept their role as someone who penetrates. If a brother meets a man who wants to penetrate, he may think it only fair that they share in the act and penetrate each other during sex." (24)

One can see the sex role confusion and gender role fluidity among Black men and its impact on the failure to be men. In this fluidity, this moral relativism reasserts itself in the Down Low homosexual subculture with its interchangeable gender roles and behavior. When reflecting back on the hyper-masculine image many Black men perpetuate, the idea of violence toward or engaging in sex with other men that act or appear submissive or passive supports Pettigrew's idea that many young Black males initially identify with their mothers, yet struggle with their masculine gender role and responsibilities. Within the Black community, the worse thing a Black male can be is the proverbial "bitch," the weak or passive individual who gets used and abused regardless of their sex. Prison culture is allowing fluidity of gender roles by saying only those that are penetrated during sex are homosexual.

In these men's minds they are not gay per say, only the person in the submissive position of reception is gay. Or as J.L. King says the men may go back and forth sharing in the penetration act.

This fulfilling of sex roles via homosexuality destroys the idea that it is anything more than a chosen behavior. These men's choices to swap sex roles but still assign masculine and feminine parameters, makes the homosexual "born gay" idea bunk. These men choose their role depending upon the moral relevance of the situation.

Homosexuality is a behavior that does nothing to enhance or sustain a community. Nor do men who participate in bisexual or homosexual behavior put forth an image that reflects the level of responsibility or self-sacrifice necessary to sustain a family, much less community. It reinforces the hypersexual image of the Black male who disregards responsibility in his quest for sex. Homosexuality is simply sex without responsibility, but there are serious consequences such as HIV. Bisexuality or homosexuality cannot be tolerated. If a man engages in any kind of sexual contact with another man, he is exhibiting homosexual behavior. The consequences of this behavior are too dire for the community to continue to ignore, embrace, or tolerate.

In the end, it is the responsibility of Black males to cease from the behavior.

As adults, these men must realize that life is not centered around them. They have failed to learn this very important lesson of manhood, that family and community are more important than your personal goals, inclinations, and needs. What many people fail to realize with males in general is that they must learn to be selfless to be a man. You cannot think about yourself and lead a family or community. Self and manhood are really incompatible. Even the soldier realizes he may have to lay down his life for his unit's objective to get accomplished. He realizes it's about the mission, not about him, though he is a necessary part of the mission. Young Black males have never been taught this lesson, nor shown how to implement it. Black men are not being responsible for the women that they impregnate, infect, and neglect. This selfish behavior is currently responsible for destroying what was Black America.

REPLACING ARCHETYPES & REDEFINING MANHOOD

Black masculinity must be redefined. A conscious shift from dependence, misogyny and violence to independence, education, and responsibility must occur. There are efforts of this sort already active within the community. Coach Ken Carter did this on an individual level when he held his students accountable for their actions while also emphasizing education over athletics. Another program is the Amer-I-can program run by Jim Brown. The Amer-I-Can program seeks to create economic empowerment through small service oriented businesses. This program seeks to build the individual self esteem of Black males so that it can be transferred to the larger community.

Older male leadership must aid in this consciousness shift. This shift will not work with outside help from the state and federal level. This is especially true when attempting to counter the gang culture which requires the older males to assert more authority over the young males to control and eventually diffuse the violence. Young Black males must not be allowed to form social groups that are outside of the larger community because it contributes to an extended adolescence. The Black community must bypass the concept of the teenager and develop young males directly from childhood to adulthood, thereby replacing the gang social order and re-integrating Black males into the Black community as productive young men who could later become husbands, fathers, and providers. They have to be guided into adulthood by men, not by devout gang members and members of their own peer group that demonstrate natural but misguided leadership ability. Many young males have no idea how to deal with adversity, disappointment, failure, and frustration other than through physical violence. The only way they will learn these life lessons is from positive leadership from within the communities in which they live.

All heterosexual Black males age 30 should fulfill some leadership position within the community, even if it's just their own family. These older males must become genuine archetypes to their communities in mass and begin to change the collective conscious image of Black masculinity.

As the ideal of Black masculinity changes through action, the underlying social and psychological issues can begin to be dealt with among the men. Black women cannot assist in this transition; it must be a male implemented movement that allows for the replacement of the street culture with a well-rounded view of Black manhood as defined by Black men. The Black female cheering, supporting, or encouraging will not benefit this movement. Black males need to recreate a patriarchal society not based on the old narcissistic southern White and Black males of film and literature, but one where the protection and maintenance of the community is the primary goal, first in nuclear families, then in neighborhoods. The narrow idea of the brute/nigger/thug/athlete must be buried by Black males without any outside interference. Eventually, the ability to provide, protect, teach, and therefore lead healthy families will be possible.

CONSPICIOUS CONSUMPTION

The Federal government is now borrowing about 2.5 billion dollars a day from foreign lenders just to operate. Currently, American wealth is assessed under the idea of ever increasing equity and credit worthiness. This wealth is not liquid and readily available, but tied up in various products such as home mortgages, car loans, 401k plans, and various pensions. This increased equity has allowed many Americans to use borrowing to temporarily raise their standard of living through refinancing of these so called investments. The Federal Reserve banking system has purposely made it easy for people to borrow more money on a revolving basis than they can ever pay back. This equity extraction increases a person's debt load, but allows them to engage in conspicuous consumption with their purchases of depreciating consumer goods. People now equate their wealth with their credit beacon score. This current American lifestyle is one of "Conspicuous Consumption." On the March 5, 2006 in the Berkshire Hathaway annual report, Warren Buffett wrote:

> As time passes, and as claims against us grow, we own less and less of what we produce. In effect, the

rest of the world enjoys an ever-growing royalty on American output. Here, we are like a family that consistently overspends its income. As time passes, the family finds that it is working more and more for the "finance company" and less for itself.. This annual royalty paid to the world - which would not disappear unless the U.S. massively under consumed and began to run consistent and large trade surpluses - would undoubtedly produce significant political unrest in the U.S. Americans would still be living very well, indeed better than now because of the growth in our economy. But they would chafe at the idea of perpetually paying tribute to their creditors and owners abroad. A country that is now aspiring to an "Ownership Society" will not find happiness in - and I'll use hyperbole here for emphasis - a "Sharecropper's Society." But that's precisely where our trade policies, supported by Republicans and Democrats alike, are taking us." (1)

Governmental Accounting Office Chief David M. Walker conducted a speaking tour to warn U.S. Citizens about the eminent financial crisis that will befall a bankrupt nation. The October 28, 2006 AP News article states:

To show that the looming fiscal crisis is not a partisan issue, he brings along economist and budget analysts from across the political spectrum. In Austin, he's accompanied by Diane Lim Rogers, a liberal economist from the Brookings Institution, and Alison Acosta Fraser, director of the Roe Institute for Economic Policy Studies at the Heritage Foundation, a conservative think tank. "We all agree on what the choices are and what the numbers are," Fraser says. Their basic message is this: If the United States government conducts business as usual over the next few decades, a national debt that is already $8.5 trillion could reach $46 trillion or more, adjusted for inflation. That's almost as much as the total net worth of every person in America, Bill Gates, Warren Buffett and those Google guys included. A hole that big could paralyze the U.S. economy; according to some projections, just the interest payments on a debt that big would be as much as all the taxes the government collects today. (2)

America's choice to live beyond its means is about to bring in the sharecropper society that Buffett describes. Sharecropping originated after the Civil War. It was a system in which a laborer and landowner split the earnings from the crops grown on a piece of land. The unfairness of the system arises from the laborer's need for housing, equipment, and seed. In sharecropping agreements, the landowner would advance credit to the laborer against his anticipated share of the crop. The laborer farms all year and at harvest time the crop is sold and the profit is split. In this profit sharing, the landowner then deducts the cost of housing, equipment, seed, and any necessities advanced on credit by the landowner. The landowner also set the price on the goods bought on credit and attached interest to the total balance. Typically, the laborer ended up with no profit after deductions because he borrowed more than his share of crop earned. He was then forced to borrow against the next year's crop to survive until the next fall. It was revolving debt that the laborer could never payoff. America is in this same pattern of borrowing against next year's tax revenue to pay for old obligations. America is borrowing against the tax revenue collected from its laborers every April 15th to pay its lenders. But the tax revenue is never enough, because politicians spend more than all U.S. Tax money collected. They borrow the difference in a daily revolving debt cycle that continually increases the level of debt. This means we as a nation will make the transition from conspicuous consumers to sharecroppers and to a much lower standard of living. By continually borrowing, we are giving away the hard assets of the nation for short term cash and consumption.

This image of fiscal irresponsibility affects a large percentage of the working/middle class. In this great wealth transfer that is taking place, Black Americans still struggle for inclusion in an economic model that is now changing for the worse, yet was never really open to them. Black Americans have less real wealth in 2007 than a century ago. In 1910, Black Americans owned more farmland than at any time before or since — at least 15 million acres. Nearly all of it was in the South, largely in Mississippi, Alabama and the Carolinas, according to the U.S. Agricultural Census. Today, Blacks own only 1.1 million of the country's more than 1 billion acres of arable land. (3) Black Americans have thrown away prime opportunities to grow businesses within the Black community because of pretense. Carter G. Woodson wrote in 1933:

> In the schools of business administration Negroes are trained exclusively in the psychology and economics of Wall Street and are, therefore, made to despise the opportunities to run ice wagons, push banana carts, and sell peanuts among their own people. Foreigners, who have not studied economics but have studied Negroes, take up this business and grow rich. (4)

The Black middle class has been groomed to be an employee and not an entrepreneur. Middle class Blacks with education have made the mistake of seeking employment with large corporations at the end of America's economic expansion. Globalization is making white collar jobs and middle manager positions obsolete. Outsourcing has allowed corporations to conduct business for 1/10 of what it costs to employ an American worker. This transition began in the 1970s with manufacturing and trade jobs being shifted overseas. Globalization is now cutting a swath through the White collar sector. By taking the carrot of the Civil Rights legislation and seeking inclusive employment, Black America has bypassed many opportunities to build real wealth. Even today, many Blacks sneer at small business ventures such as janitorial, retail, trades, and other service oriented business for the status associated with a title and salary from corporate America. Woodson wrote:

> It is unfortunate, too, that the educated Negro does not understand or is unwilling to start small enterprises which make the larger ones possible. If he cannot proceed according to the methods of gigantic corporations about which he reads in books, he does not know how to take hold of things and organize the communities of the poor along lines of small businesses. (5)

Desegregation was an opportunity for the Black middle class to distinguish themselves from the poor Black masses. They had always seen themselves as the elite who were stifled within segregated cities and towns. Desegregation allowed them to show middle class America that they were just like anybody else and deserved to be included in mainstream society. In the Black middle class mind, they felt that socializing with White society would eliminate their identification with the Black, poor, and uneducated masses.

Within the Black community, the appearance of wealth and prosperity is everything. Cars, clothes, and homes, are status symbols. This appearance of wealth and prosperity without any hard assets came solely through the extension of credit. Their homes are mortgaged, their cars are financed up to seven years, and credit cards make up the difference for clothing and jewelry. Today, being in an overpriced McMansion with an ARM or 40 year interest-only mortgage is not simply a symbol of prosperity, but is considered an investment. Whenever an event or vacation comes up, many people refinance the house, take out a little equity, and spend away. The Black middle class of the Civil Rights generation sought access to the American economic model and not independence. Carter G. Woodson wrote:

> "It is most pathetic to see Negroes begging others for a chance as we have been doing recently." Do not force us into starvation," we said. "Let us come into your stores and factories and do a part of what you are doing to profit by our trade." The Negro as a slave developed this fatal sort of dependency; and, restricted mainly to menial service and drudgery during nominal freedom, he has not grown out of it. (6)

The opportunity to engage in "conspicuous consumption," is a term used by both Carter G. Woodson and E. Franklin Frazier to describe the motivations and activities of the Black bourgeoisie. During the great migration from the south, there was a shift in the make-up and value systems of the Black middle class from the mulatto tradition to a group that would be best described as "new money." The new Black bourgeoisie was an education/money based ascendancy; the old Black bourgeoisie was culturally based.

E. Franklin Frazier wrote:

> The break with traditional values is seen in the changes in the canons of respectability. Among the older upper-class families in the Negro community, who really stood for the middle class way of life, the canons of respectability required a stable family life and conventional sex behavior. On the other hand, among the new Black bourgeoisie these values were regarded as "old fashioned" virtues and there is much confusion in thinking and behavior with reference to these values. Divorces and scandals in family and sex behavior do not affect one's social status; rather the notoriety which one acquires in such cases adds to one's prestige. The change in attitudes towards the "old fashioned" bourgeoisie values is due largely to the fact in the Negro population among whom these virtues never existed and that money has become the chief requirement for social acceptance. (7)

Frazier's statement may explain the present day trends of high illegitimacy, unstable family structures, and the continued alienation and arrested development of the Black male. The new Black bourgeoisie, empowered by education and greater economic opportunity, still exhibit the same behavioral characteristics of the masses from which they sprung. As the new Black bourgeoisie acquired middle class status, they did not reform their behavior and thinking to reflect traditional middle class mores. In that failure, the new Black bourgeoisie embraced the counterculture of White America with its promotion of the sexual revolution and drug culture which simply reinforced behavioral stereotypes that previously represented a minority of the Black community. The social shame associated with such behavior has fallen away, and as a consequence all rates of illegitimacy, divorce, and overall sexual behavior have tripled since the early 1960s. The Black community does have better employment opportunities, but at the same time it has more single parent households. This indicates an overall breakdown of the Black nuclear family unit. The new Black bourgeoisie's embracing of money as an equalizer corresponds to the Bling-Bling mentality within the Black community. Frazier states:

> Wealth to them means spending money without any reference to its source. Hence, their behavior generally reflects the worst qualities of the gentlemen and the peasant from whom their only vital traditions spring. (8)

THE QUEST FOR RESPECT

Frazier wrote about the Black bourgeoisie and their obsession with money and status:

> For they have been taught that money will bring them justice and equality in American life, and they propose to get money." (9)

Many Black Americans felt money could buy acceptance and equality. What it really bought was a certain amount of tolerance. In a May 2005 Essence Magazine article, Shelia Johnson, a Black billionaire, assumed she would be embraced by a wealthy White community. She was mistaken in the assumption that wealth would bring equality and acceptance. Shelia Johnson states:

> I have a new project now: building the Salamander Inn & Spa, which should open in 2006. The challenge is facing the opposition and the ensuing tension within the Middleburg, Virginia, commu-

nity. A handful of people were very vocal about their feelings that my project would change the character of this old-money, aristocratic town in Virginia hunt country. They don't ever want change, and they think they're right. And I feel I'm right. I have land rights, and I can put what I want on it. But we've been getting some nasty, racist mail sent to our local paper. One letter addressed to the editor said, "Get out of Virginia, you low-class nigger lover, and take Sheila with you." My daughter had a run-in with a woman at a nail salon who screamed at her, "What kind of mother do you have? You all need to leave." She got frightened and called me and said, "This woman has gone crazy on me." When it started happening, it was very hurtful and I didn't think I was going to get through it. My mother asked me, "Sheila, if you had known you would have this much resistance, would you have done it?" And I think yes. With the inn and spa, I'm laying out my vision, what I'm all about. (10)

A news article from August 22, 2006 reported that a realty company, Coldwell Banker, was found to have discriminated against potential Black buyers. Coldwell Banker realtors limited the number of properties available for showing even when prospective buyers were more than qualified to buy. One representative also told one prospective buyer to rent rather than buy in neighborhoods such as Lincoln Park, Gold Coast, and Lakeview. (11)

Many Blacks assumed that money would provide the necessary entree into White society. Recently in the Washington Post, the Rapper Jay-Z wanted to boycott Cristal because of the comments of the maker of the champagne, when "Rouzard implied the popularity of Cristal in the hip-hop community was not consistent with the image he wanted for the brand."(12) Money does not buy respect. Black Americans must give up this quest for respect and validation by White America. Frazier refers to this idea as the delusion of wealth.

> Moreover, the attraction of the delusion of wealth is enhanced by the belief that wealth will gain them acceptance in American life. In seeking an escape in the delusion of wealth, middle-class Negroes make a fetish of material things or physical possessions." (13)

The Black bourgeoisie cannot continue to waste its time pandering to a population that does not want their patronage. Such efforts are counterproductive and reflect a deep seated inferiority complex. This proving oneself equal or worthy of acceptance is to judge one's self by external standards. In the end, whatever vocation, business, or area of expertise one chooses, one must do it for the sake of the venture and for one's own knowledge and enjoyment. Excellence comes from fulfilling one's own passions and pursuits. Be the best at what you do for your own sake. Life is too short to waste your life seeking the validation of other men.

Many other minorities come to America and prosper in their chosen fields without the feeling that they have something to prove. We see this with African, Asian, Indian, Arab, and most recently Latino immigrants who bring a cultural base with them. They seek the economic opportunities that America has to offer without cultural assimilation. Most of these groups immigrated after desegregation and have no experience with traditional White American culture. Many of these minority groups want nothing to do with White Americans unless it is business oriented. Many come from colonized nations, yet they still retained their culture and identity. This can be seen with the Latino immigration movement and their blatant disregard for the White American social order. The family structure, the language barrier, and community cohesion are all an insular mechanism that is forcing White America for the first time in its history to accommodate a minority group on its own terms. This accommodation is beginning to anger many upper and middle class Whites. Unlike Black Americans, White America's affirmation and social acceptance is not necessary in fostering the minority group's identity. They brought their identity with them and do not care if White Americans accept them. These groups are concerned with building real wealth while minimizing the effects of White assimilation. The Black American on the other hand, is still not fully accepted even with the money, the education, and sacrifice to agendas that are contrary to the best interests of the Black community. Thomas Pettigrew wrote about this sting of rejection:

> Highly organized minority groups with their own cultures, who are neither fully accepted by the general society nor seeking acceptance, typically do not disparage the majority; they ignore it, if possible. It is precisely because Negro Americans are fully acculturated, desperately want full acceptance, and are denied this acceptance, that hostility against Whites is generated. (14)

Other minority groups do not carry the need to refute White America's perception of them. These minority groups do not carry the mentality of a conquered people, and so they do not feel inferior. The Black American identity is a White American construct, dictated by White America's legal, business, and social structure. This need for White acceptance is another aspect of Black America's problem.

CANNIBAL ECONOMICS AND RACIAL GATEKEEPERS

In their rejected quest to be "liked" by White America they have turned to exploiting the masses. Carter G. Woodson wrote:

> Denied participation in the higher things of life, the "educated" Negro himself joins, too, with ill-designing persons to handicap his people by systematized exploitation. Feeling the case of the Negro is hopeless, the "educated" Negro decides upon the course of personally profiting by whatever he can do in using these people as a means to an end. He grins in their faces while "extracting money" from them, but his heart shows no fond attachment to their despised cause." (15)

This exploitation does seem to draw some parallels to the current affects of outsourcing in America. Globalization has allowed corporations to increase profits by laying off the U.S. worker/consumer that formally made the product, then having it manufactured abroad for about 10% of the previous cost of production, then selling it back to American consumers at the same price as before, who now have to finance the purchase because they have less disposable income. Eventually, the U.S. consumer will be tapped out and no longer able to buy with either disposable income or financing. Globalization is allowing corporations to devour their consumer base in a cannibalistic fashion for short term profits. But long term, this will force corporations to look for other consumer markets versus maintaining a symbiotic economic relationship with consumers via livable wages and smaller profit margins.

Cannibal economics can be seen in the Black community in the drug trade. Drug use and selling have gutted the

Black community's ability to survive. Crack cocaine use increased incarceration rates, increased the number of children in foster care, and further weakened struggling family units. Crack cocaine destroyed what little community cohesion that the Black community had. Many drug dealers did not realize that what they sold had larger consequences than just one person deciding to use drugs. That person's decision and ability to use drugs affected many other people over generations.

The goal of a drug dealer is to extract as much wealth as possible from drug addicts until they die, then look for another drug addicted consumer to replace that lost revenue. The choice to sell drugs lines up with Woodson's quote above, but these men and women came from the masses rather than the educated Blacks. This is street culture and cannibal economics. The drug trade, like globalization, destroys the sustainability of a community. All one has left is young men controlling the streets by fear and intimidation.

They now sell the products of drugs, sex, and lately, a brand of street culture packaged as Hip-Hop. Stereotypes make money and so street culture is profitable right now, but like globalization, the wealth is concentrated in the hands of a few businessmen, while the community/consumer base withers away. The young emulate this culture and economic model. As did the Black bourgeoisie flee the masses with desegregation, so do the intelligent, driven individuals who happen to have been born in poverty. Individuals exploit the community and leave. Few give any thought to revitalization of their own communities, yet are angered by the White gentrification that is overtaking many U.S. cities.

From Preachers to community outreach leaders, to pimps, and drug dealers, the system of exploitation is the same. Many use the masses to build a personal financial foundation that is not funneled back into the community.

These preachers, politicians, and community outreach organizations are simply parasites. There are no depths to the depravity Black leadership will stoop to exploit the Black community. Black magazines routinely run articles about Black preachers and politicians showing how comfortably they live off of Black money in the form of tithes, offerings, and charitable donations to their non-profit enterprises. Socially, pimps, drug dealers, politicians, and preachers are all on the same level. Carter G. Woodson calls such people racial racketeers:

> This "racial racketeer" might be a politician, minister, teacher, director of a community center, or head of a "social uplift agency." As long as he did certain things and expressed the popular opinion on questions he lacked nothing, and those who followed him found their way apparently better paid as the years went by. His leadership, then, was recognized and the ultimate undoing of the Negroes in the community was assured. (16)

These "racial racketeers" have wooed segments of the Black population into following their dictates that can be sold as voting blocks to any politician. Yet these institutions are financed by the very people they exploit. E. Franklin Frazier wrote:

> The Black bourgeoisie in the United States has subsisted off the crumbs of philanthropy, the salaries of public servants, and what could be squeezed from the meager earnings of Negro workers." (17)

Most Black organizations do not work in the best interest of Black Americans. They are racial gatekeepers. These are not grassroots-based Black organizations. Though they are funded in part by the people they exploit, they generally survive off of grants and donations from the very system they are suppose to confront on social issues. In a two party system, these gatekeeper organizations maintain a certain amount of control over the population. First, it also allows the charlatan leadership leverage and justification for funding by agreeing to steer the Black populace in whatever direction the political winds may blow. Second, it provides the illusion of racial progress through photo-ops and congressional hearings. Carter G. Woodson wrote:

> Leadership is usually superimposed for the purpose of "directing the course of ostracized group along sane lines. (18)

This is why a host of Black pundits are allowed access to the American political system. Quite frankly, they are 21st century house Negroes charged with keeping control of the Negro masses. The pro-Black individuals and organizations publicly empathize with the masses, while privately catering to whatever political machine is currently in power for personal gain. On the other hand, you have the colorblind society pundits that vehemently state that race is not an issue, that Black suspicion is simply over-sensitivity, paranoia, and victimization. Neither side is designed for real change, but to preserve the status quo. Racial drama and airtime is the way to federal and philanthropic funding. Katrina victims, cop shootings, and affirmative action are issues that help these "racial racketeers" ramp up federal funding and independent donations. You rarely hear of these organizations helping minorities litigate equal employment, better living conditions, and educational improvement. Why do most of these organizations spend most of their time begging for funding from philanthropic organizations and the dues of poor Blacks? Why do none of these organizations run off of self-funding endowments that would allow them to operate independently?

One only has to investigate a bit to find that most Black organizations spend most of their revenue on high administrative costs such as payroll for bloated executive salaries. Real change and empowerment would render them unnecessary. As long as Black Americans can be steered as a voting block based on the say of such pundit leadership, we will not see change. The American political system has simply provided Black America with leadership in which White America feels comfortable. Carter G. Woodson wrote:

> The oppressor must have some dealing with the despised group, and rather than have contact with individuals he approaches the masses through his own spokesman. (19)

AN AVERSION TO LEARNING

It's been said that if you want to hide something from a nigger, put it in a book. This aversion to learning is unique to Black America. Dr. John McWhorter's book, "Losing The Race," covers the reluctance, specifically of Black Americans to delve into intellectual pursuits. He found that most Blacks of African and Caribbean descent did not have the same aversion to learning that surfaces across socioeconomic levels among Black Americans. John McWhorter wrote:

> They have a spontaneous disinclination to embrace school whole-heartedly, because it is inherent to the culture they have been immersed in since birth, long before they were part of a "peer group," to consider school a "White" and therefore alien realm (regardless of class). (20)

Black America falls into two groups, neither valuing education. The Black bourgeoisie is largely an alliterate society, a group that can read, but chooses not to. The Black bourgeoisie fills its time with gossip columns, dime novels, and information about conspicuous consumption through radio and television. E. Franklin Frazer wrote:

> The Black bourgeoisie, especially the section which forms Negro "society," scarcely ever reads books for recreation. Consequently, their conversation is trivial and exhibits a childish view of the world. (21)

The masses on the other hand, are an illiterate group. In an illiterate society, one's perception is limited to their surrounding, upbringing, and media influences. With the fragmentation of families, upbringing has less of a role in one's self perception than their surroundings and media influences. African-American history and culture is being lost and replaced with street culture based on sex, violence, money, and conspicuous consumption. Education in such communities does not immediately help to raise a standard of living. The masses are fully integrated into instant gratification which does not require long hours of study, hard work, and personal integrity. Education is seen as something to do when you can't get creditability and respect on the street. But in many situations, long term education goals do not meet the immediate needs of every day survival. For some, the basic needs of survival need to be met before education can become a priority. In other situations, where the basic needs are met, it may simply be a problem of personal initiative and motivation.

Overall, education and scholarship are not seen as something to broaden one's personal growth. It is a means to obtain the knowledge needed to acquire an income-generating job that would allow them to engage in conspicuous consumption. E. Franklin Frazier wrote:

> Education from the standpoint of fundamental culture has completely lost its significance. There is still certain snobbishness in regard to one's occupation, but the most important thing about one's income is the amount of income which it brings. (22)

Education is seen as a way to improve one's own lot in life at the expense of the community that he exploits. We see this problem in many urban school districts, which are run by a high percentage of "poverty pimps," whom appear to be highly educated. They have no solutions for the high drop out rates, the poor schooling techniques of the children, nor any interest in confronting the aversion to learning. They simply manage an ever growing problem while petitioning for more money, or stretching what little funding they do receive. There is now a standard procedure in public schools to track the few students who do stand out academically and simply warehouse the rest. In doing this, they doom students that may not be college material, but may find fulfillment in other pursuits if they received a basic education in reading, writing, and arithmetic. Yet, the Black bourgeoisie can't even provide this service to their own children. But such individuals never sought to uplift the race. They've carved a niche for themselves in white America as race experts on African-American subjects and issues while neglecting the very real problems now affecting Black America.

CONCLUSION

In the rural south of the late 1940s', White farmers began to mechanize their farms and did away with the sharecropping system that had existed since the end of the civil war. Unemployed farm hands now found themselves evicted from farms that no longer found their physical labor necessary. They began to migrate to cities to find factory work and in some instances succeeded, but generally were restricted from joining trade unions. In the 1970's, the deindustrialization of America began, and manufacturing and trades that paid living wages went with them. Currently in America, many cities have joined the information age/ service economy and have begun urban gentrification projects. The world is readjusting and Black America is not ready. In the future, manual labor, blue collar, and high tech jobs will be performed by some mechanical, automated, or robotic innovation that will render human power obsolete.

Computer scientist Billy Joy wrestled with this problem in his article, "Why the future doesn't need us," in which he discusses a book by Ray Kurzweil, entitled "The Age Of Spiritual Machines," which discusses the physical merging of man and machine via computer and robotic technology. He notes that Kurzweil discussed the very real argument of the Unabomber who wrote in his manifesto that:

> Due to improved techniques the elite will have greater control over the masses; and because human work will no longer be necessary the masses will be superfluous, a useless burden on the system. (23)

Though he and I both abhorred the Unabomber's actions, Theodore Kaczynski's argument is strong. How this affects Black America as well as the world is that large numbers of people are no longer necessary to accomplish large scale tasks. The elimination of manufacturing jobs that paid a living wage began in the 1970s'. Service jobs traditionally held by Blacks in the American working class are now held by a large Latino migration wave who compensate for these low wage jobs by consolidating households and holding multiple low wage jobs. In the future, even the Latino service worker will not be necessary. These assertions are in line with what Carter G. Woodson also saw as an automated future with little need for manual labor. In 1933 he wrote:

> In the economic order of tomorrow there will be little use for the factotum or scullion. Man will not need such personal attention when he can buy a machine to serve him more efficiently. The menial Negroes, the aggregate of parasites whom the "highly educated" Negro has exploited, will not be needed on tomorrow. What, then, will become of "our highly educated" Negroes who have no initiative." (24)

We have a Black middle class that has somewhat integrated itself into mainstream America, but we do not have the economic power or education necessary to adjust to the rapid changes in technology. In the above quote by Dr. Woodson, the Black leadership will no longer be needed in America as gatekeepers. The host of the parasitic educated Negro is dying off due to low birthrates, marriage rates, and the failure to educate future generations. A declining population means a loss in voting power, and therefore no political clout. What will the poor educated Negroes do? They will have to become experts in something other then Black theology or Black politics where they may actually produce something of value.

Now the Latino immigration wave is rising. As they move, they develop businesses within their communities, build wealth, and maintain community cohesion. On the other hand, Black Americans have failed to develop sustainable business models that build communities. They sought assimilation on the fringes of White society as employees rather than concentrate on small business and community development. Currently, Black America is now a third-tier population group as we come full circle, less the traits of self-reliance, self- discipline, nuclear families, education, and owned assets. We will in the future be worse off than our ancestors in 1900. Overt racism will resurface due to increasing immigration, U.S. economic instability, and the declining power of the federal government. Many Black Americans may not agree with this assessment, but our failure to educate our youth, the disintegrating Black family, and our cultural abhorrence to learning makes our future tenuous. We have no one to blame but ourselves for our current predicament. In the coming years, the Black American population will continue to decline and its remnants will probably disappear into the larger European and Latino populations. Carter G. Woodson wrote:

> The Negro must now do for himself or die out as the world undergoes readjustment. (25)

We have failed to learn to do for self and the price of that failure is the Death of Black America.

A SPIRITUAL EXODUS

Numbers 11:4-6
⁴And the mixed multitude among them [the rabble who followed Israel from Egypt] began to lust greatly [for familiar and dainty food], and the Israelites wept again and said, Who will give us meat to eat? ⁵ We remember the fish we ate freely in Egypt and without cost, the cucumbers, melons, leeks, onions, and garlic. ⁶But now our soul (our strength) is dried up; there is nothing at all [in the way of food] to be seen but this manna. (1)

As did the Israelites of old, neither does Black America understand the concept of freedom, nor its cost. Black America has been kept on the fringes of a larger culture, lusting after the things it offered. You hear no end to the request for better jobs, better schools, better homes, better cars, and other creature comforts. Modern Black America does not want true freedom as defined by the dictionary which means, the power to determine action without restraint. Black America wanted freedom to consume, nothing more. As did the Israelites, who only cried out from slavery when it became overly harsh, many Americans in general embrace forms of slavery in exchange for the opportunity to consume. The Israelites were provided manna from heaven that they simply had to pick up and make into bread, but they loved what they'd left in Egypt more than freedom. Slavery to them provided a sense of security and certainty about what the future held. It was written in Numbers 11:5, "We remember the fish we ate freely in Egypt and without cost, the cucumbers, melons, leeks, onions, and garlic."

They forgot to factor in the killing off of male offspring, whippings, and making brinks without straw, and punishment for not meeting their quotas. Nothing in this life is free, you pay a price for every decision you make. The Israelites did not want the God of their forefathers, but simply sustenance and comfort in exchange for labor. This is the same slave mindset that requires a spiritual exodus for Black America. An exodus means a going out: a departure or emigration. God called Moses and Aaron to lead his people out of Egypt into the land he had promised to Abraham. God honored his Word to Abraham and Exodus was the act to demonstrate the fulfillment of that promise. But quite simply, the Israelites feared the Egyptians more than God as demonstrated in Exodus 14:8-12:

> [8]The Lord made hard and strong the heart of Pharaoh king of Egypt, and he pursued the Israelites, for [they] left proudly and defiantly. [9]The Egyptians pursued them, all the horses and chariots of Pharaoh and his horsemen and his army, and overtook them encamped at the [Red] Sea by Pi- hahiroth, in front of Baal-zephon. [10]When Pharaoh drew near, the Israelites looked up, and behold, the Egyptians were marching after them; and the Israelites were exceedingly frightened and cried out to the Lord. [11]And they said to Moses, Is it because there are no

graves in Egypt that you have taken us away to die in the wilderness? Why have you treated us this way and brought us out of Egypt? ¹²Did we not tell you in Egypt, Let us alone; let us serve the Egyptians? For it would have been better for us to serve the Egyptians than to die in the wilderness. (2)

In Exodus 14:8-12, they preferred the certainty of slavery over the uncertainty of freedom and responsibility of dealing with the unknown. The Egyptians pursued them because they were initially defiant and proud, a blatant slap in the face to a former master with a superiority complex.

The Israelites told Moses that he should have left them alone to serve the Egyptians rather than the possibility of death in the wilderness. They preferred slavery over freedom because they feared death. They had learned to live with shame. They were secure in knowing their place. They preferred physical bondage over the abstract ideas of emotional and spiritual freedom. They had more faith in the Egyptian system of government than in the God that delivered them from slavery. But because God knew this spirit of fear and faith in the Egyptian, God caused the Israelites to wander in the wilderness for forty years to purge them of their old way of thinking and behaving.

Numbers 14:29-33: ²⁹Your dead bodies shall fall in this wilderness--of all who were numbered of you, from twenty years old and upward, who have murmured against Me, ³⁰Surely none shall come into the land in which I swore to make you dwell, except Caleb son of Jephunneh and Joshua son of Nun. ³¹But your little ones whom you said would be a prey, them will I bring in and they shall know the land which you have despised and rejected. ³²But as for you, your dead bodies shall fall in this wilderness. ³³And your children shall be wanderers and shepherds in the wilderness for forty years and shall suffer for your whoredoms (your infidelity to your espoused God), until your corpses are consumed in the wilderness. ³⁴After the number of the days in which you spied out the land [of Canaan], even forty days, for each day a year shall you bear and suffer for your iniquities, even for forty years, and you shall know My displeasure [the revoking of My promise and My estrangement]. ³⁵I the Lord have spoken; surely this will I do to all this evil congregation who is gathered together against Me. In this wilderness they shall be consumed [by war, disease, plagues], and here they shall die. (3)

Only Israelites under the age of twenty entered into the Promised Land. God destroyed those that would not yield to him, but instead held fast to the ways of the Egyptians and their false gods. Only those that had no direct memory of slavery and held God's ways versus the Egyptians' ways entered into the Promised Land. Black America needs a spiritual exodus, a departure, from the former mentality and behavior adopted while in its own spiritual Egypt (the American social structure) with its unconscious belief in White divinity.

WHITE DIVINITY

> **2 Corinthians 10:12** For we dare not make ourselves of the number, or compare ourselves with some that commend themselves: but they measuring themselves by themselves, and comparing themselves among themselves, are not wise. (4)

When it comes to race in America, simply being born White was justification for moral and intellectual superiority. Regardless of region, racism has and will always be a part of American society, and it will continue to be defined in term of Black and White as long as both groups coexist. But the worship of the spiritual Egyptian reflects that racist notions in society must be broken down and exposed. American Protestantism is steeped in the tradition of Aryan Christian identity groups that believe in total separation of races to protect the genetic purity of the Caucasian race. These men and women over the past four hundred years neglected to fully read their Bibles. Luke 16:15 says to justify yourselves before men is an abomination before God. The word "justify" in theological terms means to declare innocent or guiltless; absolve; acquit. What traditional Protestantism and Catholicism is saying is that Whiteness, in comparison to other races, makes them innocent, guiltless, in other words, perfect in the eyes of God. They justify this because of the supposed blessing of being born White, and therefore, blameless, and thus God's chosen people. The Jews are referred to as the offspring of Satan and people of color are called mud people. To them people of color are beasts without souls that can be conquered, killed, and abused without consequence because they are genetically outside of God's chosen Adamic seed line. This ideology is only slightly different from the Islamic idea of killing and enslaving infidels which is based more on professed belief than on race. By their argument, White Christians are the epitome of humanity; whom God has given dominion over the various beasts of the earth.

This belief system cloaked in Christianity is the founding belief of European Christianity and racism. Whiteness is godliness. When people think of themselves as divine because of their skin color and not because of their behavior, they've strayed from the basic tenet of Jesus, "Love your neighbor as you love yourself."

The White divinity complex justifies enslaving, raping, killing, and suppressing supposed sub-humans under the belief that their submission is necessary to maintain the genetic integrity and superiority of the White race. In the American south, this is reflected in the attitudes of White men that fathered bastard mulatto children. They believed that infusions of White genetics into lesser peoples improved sub-humans. Granted this was only tolerated from White males to sub-human females. This breeding up process supposedly added an increased intellectual ability that supposedly explains the slightly higher IQ scores of Black Americans.

White men's rape and exploitation of darker women was seen as a blessing in the form of mulatto children. The infusion of Whiteness removed them if only by percentage points from the root of sin, that of simply being a Black African or some other dark race. U. S. Senator Bilbo wrote:

> We have already determined that the Negro race is physically, mentally, and morally inferior to the White race, and those who accept this comparison can readily see the dangers of amalgamation. In fact, it is difficult to understand how any soberminded man can hesitate to conclude that the mingling of the inferior with the superior will result in the lowering of the higher stock. This is true of the crossing of plants, of the crossing of animals, and thousands of years of racial contact have proved that it is true of the crossing of the different races of mankind. (5)

The error of White divinity is refuted by 1 Corinthians 15:50 which states:

> Now this I say, brethren, that flesh and blood cannot inherit the kingdom of God; neither doth corruption inherit incorruption. (6)

The Bible states that no flesh and blood can inherit the kingdom of God, regardless of color because all flesh is corrupt by nature. No flesh can stand in the presence of God. God is spirit. White flesh, nor Black flesh, nor yellow flesh, nor brown flesh can inherit the kingdom of God. What White divinity has tried to do is make a spiritual issue a carnal issue with divinity determined by the color of a person's flesh. White divinity comes from the idea of the divine right of kings. The idea of divinity applied to mortals is prevalent throughout history, usually in the belief of the divine right of kings. This divine right applied to humans gave certain individuals total authority over other people.

Political leaders are known to have claimed actual divinity in certain early societies — the ancient Egyptian Pharaohs being the premier case — taking a role as objects of worship and being credited with superhuman status and powers. More commonly, and more pertinent to recent history, leaders merely claim some form of divine mandate, suggesting that their rule is in accordance with the will of God.(7)

The average White person had the power of life or death over a Black person in America. The word of a White person could grant them mercy or condemn them to death. This belief that White rule is in accordance with the will of God has set America on par with the hubris common to the protagonist of ancient Greece mythology. Hubris according to its modern usage is exaggerated self pride or self-confidence, often resulting in fatal retribution. (8)

But the fear of fatal retribution brought on by racial hubris lead to brutal means to maintain the belief in racial superiority. Such people did not realize that this hubris exposes the very flaws of their assumed God given superiority. If White people are so innately superior, why were physical slaughter, enslavement, and subjugation necessary for people thought too dumb to understand the concept of personal freedom and self-determination. Their counterpoint to this assertion is the myth of the benevolent slave master.

BENEVOLENT MASTERS

Under traditional southern Christian conservative ideology, the American caste system consisted of three classes. The first class was the slaveholding aristocracy; the second consisted of small plot farmers and poor Whites, and finally the Negro slave. The slaveholding aristocracy believed that a Negro could be improved through selective breeding and management. They believed White divinity and their innate benevolence bestowed upon them the duty to improve the Negro in both mind and body. The Negro being an amoral creature could be improved by those whose intellectual capacity surpasses that of the Negro for the benefit of White America as manual laborers. When this belief was mixed with Christian ideology and a campaign to drive out the "innate" heathen ways of the Negro with pagan White Christianity, the benevolent master ideology was most evident. The idea was to protect the Negro from himself and to make him a contributor to a superior culture even if only at menial labor. This benevolent White population felt it was their responsibility to control and manage the Black population for the maintenance of the traditional southern social order. Harriet Beecher Stowe's novel, "Uncle Tom's Cabin" countered this racist idea which drew much southern criticism.

The response to Stowe's novel in the American South was one of outrage. To counter Stowe's novel, Southern writers produced a number of proslavery books, the vast majority of them fictionalized novels. In 1852 alone, eight anti-Tom novels were published. These anti-Tom novels tended to feature a benign White patriarchal master and a pure wife, both of whom presided over child-like slaves in a benevolent extended-family-style plantation. The novels either implied, or directly stated, the racist view that African Americans were unable to live their lives without being directly overseen by White people. (9)

The idea of the benevolent master persisted after the civil war in the form of sharecropper/tenant farmer relationships. After the few gains of reconstruction, and the federal and state reestablishment of White rule in the south, the myth was retrenched in the southern psyche. The sharecropper system had all of the social advantages of slavery for Whites without the financial obligations. All of the necessities for sharecroppers were financed by benevolent masters who extended credit to Negroes who previously had no access to capital or experience in money management. Out of supposed selfless forethought and benevolence they "helped" the Negro who was no more able to care for himself now than in slavery.

THE COMPLICITY OF THE WHITE POPULATION

Despite being of low economic class, simply being White came with the birth right of superiority and control over a lower caste. The poor White population served as overseers, slave catchers, yeoman farmers, and aspiring gentry. Whiteness guaranteed them access to the upper class. Typically, the poor White population dealt with field slaves on a daily basis and acted as a buffer between the aristocracy and the slave masses. Howard Zinn wrote:

> The need for slave control lead to an ingenious device, paying poor Whites-themselves so troublesome for two hundred years of southern history- to be overseers of Black labor and therefore buffers for Black hatred. (10)

These are the people that directly administered workloads, mating changes, meted out punishment, and reported to the aristocracy the productivity of the cheap labor force. Poor Whites were given the same power and authority as the slave owning aristocracy over the Negro further supporting White divinity and the benevolent master idea. Poor Whites were given by default the belief in their innate spiritual, intellectual, and physical superiority based on skin color. This belief bonded the poor White population and the White aristocracy in a social contract for the perpetuation of White divinity.

This idea is still evident among modern day southern apologists who sit around civil war reenactments and blue gray affairs lamenting the good old days of chivalry, civility, and good Christian values. Supposedly Masters loved their Negroes and Negroes loved them. In their mind, slavery and the old south was mutually beneficial to White and Black alike. The old south is looked at as the Camelot of America. I've often heard the question posed, "What if the south had won the war?" When any person holds another innocent person in any form of involuntary servitude, the enslaver can never be referred to as good, beneficial, or benevolent.

What many of today's poor southern Whites fail to realize is their true historical social standing in relationship to the slaveholding aristocracy. This class structure is starkly drawn in the William Faulkner short story, "Wash." Wash is an aged poor White man who squats on the land of Colonel Sutpen and is his ever present sidekick. Wash believes that by association with Colonel Sutpen he is in the presence of perfection. Wash even allows the aged Colonel to have his way with his fifteen year old granddaughter believing that the Colonel would conduct himself honorably toward the young girl. This illusion is shattered on the day his granddaughter gives birth to Colonel Sutpen's child and upon seeing the child, the Colonel is more excited about a colt born that same morning than the sight of his new born daughter, and the girl he's dishonored. When Colonel Sutpen says to the Granddaughter, "Well, Milly, too bad you're not a mare. Then I could give you a decent stall in the stable." (11) Wash suddenly realizes that the Colonel has a higher regard for his horses than for Wash and his granddaughter. Wash's perception of the infallible southern aristocracy is shattered. Wash, in a fit of rage kills the Colonel to uphold his granddaughter's honor, something he felt only the upper class could have. He believed a lie and as the posse comes he sees these people, his betters, as flawed human beings no better than himself. This God-like perception of the southern aristocracy is what convinced thousands of men like Wash to go and die in the Civil War for a cause that was not in their best interest, but in the economic interest of their betters.

MODERN BENEVOLENT MASTERS

Today the belief in Black ineptness and in the need for White management infects both conservatives and liberals alike, but manifests itself in two distinct forms of social interaction. The Republican Party and its supporters generally draw from the old southern Christian ideology that Blacks have an innate animalistic tendency and lack intellect.

They believe Blacks are a danger to society if they are not properly managed. The supporters of the Republican Party are essentially modern day poor Whites aspiring to identify with the modern aristocracy. Carroll Quigley in his book, "Tragedy and Hope," describes this aspect of the population in America and its supporters.

> Above the middle class which dominated the country in the first half of the twentieth century, were a small group of aristocrats. Below were the petty bourgeoisie, who had middle-class aspirations, but were generally insecure and often bitter because they did not obtain middle class rewards." (12) The second most numerous group in the United States is the petty bourgeoisie, including millions of persons who regard themselves as middle-class and are under all the middle- class anxieties and pressures, but often earn less money than unionized laborers. As a result of these things they are often envious, filled with hatreds, and are generally the chief recruits for any Radical Right, Fascist, or hate campaigns against any group that is different or which refuses to conform to middle-class values." "Made up of clerks, shopkeepers, and vast numbers of office workers in business, government, finance, and education, these tend to regard their White-collar status as the chief value in life, and live in an atmosphere of envy, pettiness, insecurity, and frustration. They form the major portion of the Republican Party's supporters in the towns of America, as they did for the Nazis in Germany thirty years ago." (13)

It is interesting that American and Nazi racial ideologies were so similar. Like the Nazis, local, state, and the federal government used terror tactics to maintain segregation and racial superiority under the premise of White divinity. There are many local organizations across the United States still using benign sounding names and Christian slanted ideology to promote racial superiority.

It is most often an unspoken agreement, this idea of White divinity and contrived racial benevolence held by the aristocratic and poor White class that is still alive today. With a class below your own, the sting of economic and class inequity are deflated under the common cause of White divinity. But after the civil war, it was southern Black legislatures that brought about the public school system, and other social programs.

Prior to that time, poor Whites remained uneducated unless a community or individual paid to have a teacher brought to their locale. Only the slaveholding aristocracy and upper middle class received educations. Illiteracy was the norm of the day for Black and White alike. Yet, poor Whites backed the separate but equal ruling under the understanding that White public schools would receive more funding than negro/colored schools. Most upper class families sent their children to academies where they would not mingle with "White Trash," yet the racial superiority bond held across economic boundaries. This social contract is still evident today among the petty bourgeoisies that Quigley wrote about.

Today, this petty bourgeoisie class is threatened by the idea of superior productivity by darker people. Many Blacks cannot count the number of times a White petty bourgeoisie person gives them an incredulous look when they do not fit the parameters of Blackness, or seek their approval or acceptance.

When one measures themselves against the base line of a class system and doesn't measure up, it destroys the idea of racial superiority. Segregation was the remedy for this problem. By 1900, many Blacks had acquired land and were independent farmers despite racism. Knowing that they were unwanted by the larger White community, they set up Black townships in the southeast and western United States. To counter this move for economic empowerment and independence, state and federal government legislation was used to discourage such development. Segregationists did not want self determination and economic freedom. If Black America looks back at slavery, reconstruction, the Tuskegee experiments, COINTELPRO, Iran Contra, and most recently the Federal response to Hurricane Katrina, you must assume that Black America's presence is unwanted. But to allow independent Black communities would destroy the belief in White divinity and Black inability to form independent and sustainable communities.

The petty bourgeoisie continues to massage their own low self-esteem by their complicity in the destruction and subversion of others. They do not want to socialize, live, speak, or work around people that are different than themselves. They want a homogenous society. Segregation grants them this fantasy world of God-given Aryan supremacy by stifling fair competition.

In 2004, in Waynesboro, VA, Moreko Griggs, a Black male, was named Valedictorian of Waynesboro High school until the day before graduation when he was told there had been a change and new grades had come in and Griggs would be named co-valedictorian with two White students. Traditionally, the school had discounted grades from the final three weeks of classes when calculating grade-point averages at the end of the year. Honors teachers are asked only to provide an estimate of the students' final grades. (14)

This area of Virginia is quite homogenous and it's not a surprise that such a move to maintain White superiority would occur. Within this group of petty bourgeoisie, the parameters of Blackness are really no different from those of generations earlier. Blacks are thought of as sinful, liars, thieves, overly sexual, drug abusers, violent, not very bright, but athletic. White Americans that believe this are the type that love the newest football or basketball stud and their admiration of such Black men or women is akin to taking a picture with the latest Kentucky Derby Winner.

At one time, many of this group used athletics to acquire college educations. Once Black athletes were allowed into White only universities and demonstrated superior athleticism, this group conceded this ability to the Black community, but sought to maintain intellectual superiority by stating that Blacks didn't have the mind for tactics and strategy in sports events.

The time of the petty bourgeoisie/poor White population is passing away. The social contract has been void. The economic and social elite no longer need the services of race warriors in the form of the Ku Klux Klan, Christian Identity, and Neo-Nazi groups. This waning need can be seen in the federal government's current infiltration of these groups. Essentially, such people are seen as poor White trash, who no longer have a purpose or a place in what was a White/Black population. This fear that they are losing their place makes them reactionary, but they have failed to recognize the real issue of class in American society. With globalization and the outsourcing of well paying White collar and manufacturing jobs, so goes the uneven playing field of the last 400 years. China and India now produce a better educated, hardworking, lower cost labor force, each of whose middle class totally encompasses or surpasses the entire American population. Eventually, America's petty bourgeoisie/working class population will slip back into the poor White economic class of their ancestors from which they came.

THE PITY PARTY

On the other side of the benevolent master coin is the liberal. I will call those of the liberal bent members of the pity party. The liberal feels pity for Black America. This pity is crippling because it absolves the object of personal responsibility. The liberal has the same preconceived notions on race and ability, but instead of the typical loathing by the petty bourgeoisie, the liberal feels pity in that these people had the misfortune of being born Black. Due to that misfortune of being born Black, such people are saddled from the womb with inferior abilities and inclinations. The liberal feels they must accept that Blacks are inferior and help them to compensate for their lack of ability. In many ways the liberal sees being born Black as akin to being mentally retarded. This "Black Retardation" automatically lowers their expectations of Black people. Again, we are back to the parameters of Blackness. Except this time, the liberal seeks to celebrate stereotypes of Black people. The Republican Party on the other hand, simply keeps a few Black Republicans around for the appearance of diversity.

Another aspect of this racism surfaces in the Democratic Party's backing of the homosexual political strategy that uses the Civil Rights legacy as a means to gain equal protection under the law. The homosexual agenda seeks to paint itself as a minority group denied Civil Rights. This use of the Civil Rights legacy for the gain of legislation based on sexual behavior is a slap in the face to all that died asserting their rights to be treated as human beings. Homosexuality is a behavior and not a set of physical characteristics that can be defined or equated with a specific race or racial group. There are no physical characteristics of homosexuality, only behaviors that consist of various acts of sodomy. Race, on the other hand, is defined as a local, geographic, or global human population distinguished as a more or less distinct group by genetically-transmitted physical characteristics.

Homosexuals do not produce children with genetically-transmitted physical characteristics that could define them as a race.

Many in the homosexual community say they were born gay. They use the "Born Gay" premise to link their cause to the Civil Rights agenda. The homosexual community is trying to consolidate itself into a pseudo race for political gain. They seek to equate the physical condition of being Black with homosexual behavior. As long as they can be seen as a separate or distinct oppressed group, the homosexual agenda can slowly advance. To attempt to equate homosexuality with the unique physical characteristics of African descent is to pull a pseudo race card. The homosexual community is no different than the KKK or the Aryan Nation when they insinuate that to be Black is to be predisposed to certain behaviors.

The homosexual community is saying that people of African descent are predisposed to act within a framework carefully defined by instinctual urges unique to that race. They are attempting to equate race with behavior. It's akin to saying you have to act Black and you cannot help it, it's innate. The homosexual agenda wants the world to see homosexuality as a pseudo race with innate behaviors that cannot be changed. This racism limits people to narrow stereotypes such as the cheap Jew, the sneaky Asian, the dumb African, etc. This misappropriation of the Civil Rights legacy for legitimatization of sexual behavior must be confronted.

This liberal racism also finds a foothold through multiculturalism that teaches the embracing of sports, dance, and religion as things that Blacks do well that should be celebrated. It's now politically correct to explain away self destructive behavior as something inborn. It justifies the need by the pity party to protected Blacks from themselves. In this modern world, many people feel that Black Americans cannot make the intellectual leap needed to survive in a changing world. Like the benevolent master of old, liberal social programs were deemed necessary to control and manage the Black population.

The Black community should separate itself from the Democratic Party and elect officials as independents who might better serve the needs of the Black community.

The "War on Poverty," implemented by Lyndon Johnson and the social programs that followed were a band-aid for what is first a problem of economics, then of sociology. Many Blacks lived in poverty due to segregation. They were never given the opportunity to develop self-sustaining communities. Such communities were normally destroyed. Most Blacks worked in service jobs for the larger White communities for low wages. The benevolent masters of the south wanted a compliant, cheap, readily available source of manual labor. Terrorism, segregation, unequal funding of education, and restricted access to certain occupations caused poverty.

Instead of dealing with the economic inequity, welfare and public housing were programs that supported the notion of Black inferiority. These programs began to fracture economically strained families by not allowing an adult male in a household. It did allow women to receive housing and food stamps for herself and her children as long as she was unmarried. Why not subsidize housing for a fixed number of years, but require gainful employment? Years later, many Blacks feel entitled to welfare, section 8 housing, and food stamps. They have become slaves of the state. Now they line up at the welfare line instead of Mr. Charlie's plantation house for food and clothing allotments.

The pity party would have you believe that Blacks are not capable of doing for self. The pity party takes the Black population for granted because most Blacks are democrats by default. The Republican Party loathes Blacks almost as much as it does its pseudo Christian base. The pity party simply comes into Black churches around election time to kiss Black babies, and quote Martin Luther King Jr.

As long as funding for social programs keeps flowing, they assume Blacks should be satisfied since it's more than the Republican Party will do, which is absolutely nothing. The pity party has simply cloaked their White divinity in a more palatable version of the mythic benevolent master of the rural south.

SPIRITUAL SLAVES

> **Exodus 14:8-9:** [8]The Lord made hard and strong the heart of Pharaoh king of Egypt, and he pursued the Israelites, for [they] left proudly and defiantly. [9]The Egyptians pursued them, all the horses and chariots of Pharaoh and his horsemen and his army, and overtook them encamped at the [Red] Sea by Pi-hahiroth, in front of Baal-zephon. (15)

Exodus 14:8 refers to Pharaoh pursuing the Israelites because they left proudly and defiantly. This parallels the struggle for Black dignity in America. Normal human dignity has been systematically denied for generations. But in each instance where such grassroots movements began they were squelched by local, state, and federal authorities. To be proud and defiant as the Israelites was a threat to the status quo. To be independent of one's master, and to have self-respect and a sense of equality with that former master refuted the idea of personal divinity held by both Egypt's Pharaoh and by White America. Pharaoh's hubris enslaved him so thoroughly that he sent forth armies to maintain that status quo. He was as much a slave as the Israelites. He was a slave to his own self image, his perceived power, and to the past. America is a slave to her own image; her past, like Pharaoh. You are no longer Godlike when you cannot impose worship of oneself by others. Narcissistic Personality Disorder (NPD) is the sin of America. Dr. Golomb's definition of Narcissistic Personality can be applied to both the Black and White American population. Dr. Golomb defines NPD as:

> Narcissism is a psychological disorder resulting from a person's belief that he or she is flawed in a way that makes the person fundamentally unacceptable to others. This belief is held below the person's conscious awareness; such a person would typically deny thinking such a thing if questioned. In order to protect themselves against the intolerably painful rejection and isolation they imagine would follow if others recognized their supposedly defective nature, such people make strong attempts to control others' view of them and behavior towards them. (16)

By Dr. Golomb's definition, Black Americans have the converse of the white problem which is the internal belief that they are flawed by Blackness that makes them unacceptable to others. Yet, they will never admit it. They believe that the European/White American is superior. These Black Americans spend their lives attempting to change or control White America's racial perceptions of Black Americans. This group seeks acceptance from White America through imitation. But in relation to White America, the historical application of violence to control the perception of them as superior is a textbook case of the Narcissistic Personality Disorder. They have had to continually reinforce Black America's belief in White superiority through violent and legislative means. They've created a Godlike perception of themselves that must be maintained from generation to generation through violence and various forms of disenfranchisement. Black Codes, false Christianity, and Jim Crow were used to reinforce behavior and the belief in White superiority. The only reason to justify such action was to deny one's humanity and elevate their self esteem.

This same caste system is not unique; India has a similar caste system in which the dark skin Dalit people (untouchable or broken people) struggle with the upper caste to break the 3000 year old tradition of segregation based on skin color. Under this Hindu-based caste system, the Dalit have been forced to believe that it is their birthright to suffer prejudice, abuse, and mistreatment until they die. Currently, Christian missionaries have encountered resistance by the India government to converting Dalits' to Christianity which teaches equality in Jesus Christ. (17) This resistance to true Christianity is no different than the American "Christian" ideology that taught that Black people were forever outside of god's grace, that Blackness deemed them to a lifetime of physical, sexual, and psychological abuse without a possibility of deliverance. The Hindu and American Christian hold essentially the same racist ideology, which is the desire to elevate their own self-image at the expense of another's humanity. It seems the European/American Christian ideology is bunk, and has no more of the message of Jesus Christ in it than Hinduism with its idol worship of cattle and rats.

Until White America lets go of its need for control and the masking of its hypocrisy, it will continue to be a place of racial tension and anti-assimilation. White America must repent of its pride and Black America must overcome its shame. Until America repents of its hard heartedness, it will be as Pharaoh, putting time and effort into maintaining the flawed mythology of White superiority. If it does not, it will die because of its failure to repent of past deeds, turn on a new path and do what is righteous without respect of a person's physical appearance. Jesus said in Matthew 12:50

"For whoever does the will of My Father in heaven is My brother and sister and mother!" (18)

WANDERING IN A SPIRITUAL WILDERNESS

ACTS 7:35 It was this very Moses whom they had denied (disowned and rejected), saying, Who made you our ruler (referee) and judge? whom God sent to be a ruler and deliverer and redeemer, by and with the [protecting and helping] hand of the Angel that appeared to him in the bramblebush. (19)

The spiritual problem of Black America is that we choose to wander in a spiritual wilderness. It's not that we are really lost or confused; the road stands in front of us bidding us to come into the promise. But like the Israelites of old, our problem is one of simple disobedience to the teachings of Jesus Christ. Neither White nor Black America really wants the pure gospel of Jesus Christ, only an idol version that requires no internal change, but simply justifies their personal inclinations. The above quote from Stephen in the book of Acts convicted the descendents of those that disobeyed Moses. The Lord heard their cry for deliverance from the Egyptian, but they rejected who God sent and what God said to do.

God did hear the Black man's cry for deliverance for freedom and set brother against brother to die for a people whom they deemed subhuman. Half a million people died for a cause they deny, that the civil war was about each state's right to decide to be a slaveholding or a free state. Once free, we set about appealing to our former Masters (Egyptians) for equality and fairness. We did not seek our deliverer Jesus. He is our Moses, and we rejected him while still professing him with our mouths.

ACTS 7:39 [And yet] our forefathers determined not to be subject to him [refusing to listen to or obey him]; but thrusting him aside they rejected him, and in their hearts yearned for and turned back to Egypt. (20)

Many Black churches, as do many White churches, "pimp" the image of Jesus for gains of power and wealth. Few teach the practical application of the words of Jesus Christ. Instead, they promote the acquisition of goods, perform music shows, dance in trances, and glorify the authority of smooth-talking preachers whose words further enslave the hearer. Carter G. Woodson wrote:

> Those who keep the people in ignorance and play upon their emotions must be exiled. The people have never been taught what religion is, for most of the preachers find it easier to stimulate the superstition which develops in the unenlightened mind. Religion is such hands, then, becomes something with which you take advantage of weak people. Why try to enlighten the people in such matters when superstition serves just as well for exploitation? (21)

The Black community is guilty of choosing to follow leaders that keep them in bondage for gain. These leaders keep the peoples' eyes turned back to Egypt. Having been released from overt physical oppression, we turned back to Egypt with a twisted faith that awaits acceptance. Since slavery was outlawed, Black America has continually tried to turn back to America, but is rejected each time. Black America has played the whore.

Ezekiel 16: 32 But as a wife that committeth adultery, which taketh strangers instead of her husband! 33 They give gifts to all whores: but thou givest thy gifts to all thy lovers, and hirest them, that they may come unto thee on every side for thy whoredom. (22)

As the prophet Ezekiel spoke of Israel, so has Black America done unto America. We have paid the price of whoredom, but at the same time also been the whore. We've gifted our lovers with blood for the acceptance that is continually denying us while shunning the one (Jesus Christ) who loves us. Black America has fought in every war this country has engaged in to prove to our chosen masters that we are worthy of acceptance only to be shoved off into second class citizenship after each war. Black America has chosen the way of the adulterous wife, for even the common whore receives gifts, yet she is contrary to this in that she pays her lovers who abuse her. Americanism is our golden calf, an idol god that promises life, liberty, and the pursuit of happiness. The cucumbers, melons, leeks, onion, and garlic are now play stations, McMansions, expensive cars, and prestigious employment.

Exodus 32:8 They have turned aside quickly out of the way which I commanded them; they have made them a molten calf and have worshiped it and sacrificed to it, and said, These are your gods, O Israel, that brought you up out of the land of Egypt! (23)

We wrongly give praise to America for setting us free. Everyone wants to be God's chosen people, like the Israelite of old, but the Israelite is human too, and failed to enter into dependence and worship of God by applying his ways to their daily lives. The Israelites were kept in the wilderness forty years until the Egyptian slave mind died. This self will and idol worship is the work of men's hands. Doing what one wants instead of what they are called to do spiritually is sin. God judged all that did evil in his sight to die off and never enter into the promise land.

> **Numbers 32:13** And the Lord's anger was kindled against Israel and He made them wander in the wilderness for forty years, until all the generation that had done evil in the sight of the Lord was consumed. (24)

Black America is guilty of this very offense of false worship and disobedience. We did not fully seek Jesus, only physical displays of faith in dance and singing. If Black America as a people were obedient to God's Word, our families would not be in shambles, we would not be at war with our children, nor intertwined in drugs, fornication, and high HIV rates. This is due largely to the failure of the modern Black male to grow up and strive to reconstruct the nuclear family according to the teachings of Jesus Christ. All the while, church plays up the exact consumerism and Americanism that aids in this process of self-destruction. Unless Black America enters into the rest of Jesus Christ, we will continue to wander and die in this spiritual wilderness called the modern world. Psalm 95: 10-11 states:

> Forty years long was I grieved and disgusted with that generation, and I said, It is a people that do err in their hearts, and they do not approve, acknowledge, or regard My ways. 11 Wherefore I swore in My wrath that they would not enter My rest [the land of promise]. (25)

Wandering in the spiritual wilderness as an adult is a choice. No one has a choice over the circumstances that they are born into, but as an adult you have the choice as to how you will choose to live everyday. Black America wanders from promise land to promise land. From the great migration to large cities such as New York and Chicago, later to the White suburbs of the late 1960s, and now to places such as Atlanta, Washington, D.C., and Charlotte, N.C... None of these places makes the predicament of the Black community any better if individuals simply keep transplanting the same behavior from one place to another. It makes no sense to move to a new place unless you want to be a new person. Simply moving the old person to a new location wrecks the new place with the same destructive behaviors as the old one. The problem is not with the place, it is with the desire of the hearts of the individuals who move. Black Americans carry the slave identity within their hearts as did the Israelites carry Egypt's ways in their hearts. No amount of money, projects, section 8 housing, or moving to the suburbs will change the current behavior of the Black community until individuals decide to live in a different fashion and renounce (repent) their former behaviors. Until Black America ceases from its own works of urban culture, promiscuity, drug use, moral relativism, and pagan folk traditions, absolutely nothing will change within the Black community. It will only worsen.

> **Hebrews 4:11** Let us therefore be zealous and exert ourselves and strive diligently to enter that rest [of God, to know and experience it for ourselves], that no one may fall or perish by the same kind of unbelief and disobedience [into which those in the wilderness fell]. (26)

But this step would require a change, a letting go of America and relying on the one true Lord, Jesus Christ. No moving away to White neighborhoods or different countries and starting fresh will fix this problem of reluctance to accept Jesus as Lord and Savior. No social program can stop a people bent on fornication, adultery, violence, and self destruction. Some believe spiritually that they are nothing more than sub-human descendents of slaves. Neither Americanism nor Afrocentrism will help us, for it was our African brothers who sold us to America for guns and rum. Wearing kinte cloth and dancing around trees with chicken blood won't create the change of heart needed to evolve and live. If Afrocentrism and African beliefs worked, Africa would not be stuck in the tribalism, paganism, and superstition that are decimating the continent.

America's spiritual wilderness entangles us in the cycle of a sinful, narcissistic society. The sad fact is that Black America has more faith in America's ability to deliver happiness than in Jesus. Black America remains stuck in humanism when what is necessary to overcome the problems of society is to become spiritual rather than carnal. Carnality and its physical stimulation override many people's spiritual inclinations to behave on a higher level. On an individual level, people will have to be born again and filled with the Holy Spirit in order to find deliverance from the problems that plague individuals and society.

The problem is that no one wants to leave the physical parameters of their life and physical things that they love more dearly than Jesus Christ. The change required of giving up physical comforts for the responsibilities and physical restrictions of spirituality based in Jesus Christ is too much to ask for some individuals.

Individuals regardless of color must leave spiritual Egypt and go forward into the promise of Jesus Christ. Know that when you refuse the teachings of Jesus, that you have made a choice to wander and struggle in this spiritual wilderness called the world. For that choice, you will eventually encounter eternal damnation and separation from God, but while you draw breath, know that your present separation from God is by choice.

In the end, if individual change does not occur, then there is no justification for complaining about one's personal or community's predicament. A choice has been made to participate in the American social order. This participation in the American experience requires Black America to fulfill racial roles defined by people spiritually no better off than themselves. The White American is not God, nor is he superior to any other man, and deep down he knows this. Jesus said in Luke 16:15:

> And he said unto them, Ye are they which justify yourselves before men; but God knoweth your hearts: for that which is highly esteemed among men is abomination in the sight of God. (27)

ENDNOTES

I. THE DEATH OF BLACK AMERICA

(1) Save America Ministries. A Portrait of the Black Family: 2005 V. Accessed December 2, 2006.http://www.saveus.org/docs/factsheets/portrait_Black_family7-12-05.pdf

(2) Quigley, Carroll. Tragedy And Hope: A History of the world in our Time. New York: The Macmillan Company, 1966. p.1287.

(3) Jones, Joy. "Marriage Is for White People". Washington Post. March 26, 2006. B1

(4) Moynihan, Daniel Patrick. The Negro Family: The Case For National Action. Office of Policy Planning and Research United States Department of Labor. 1965.

(5) Save America Ministries. A Portrait of the Black Family: 2005 V. Accessed December 2, 2006. <http://www.saveus.org/docs/factsheets/portrait_Black_family7-12-05.pdf>

(6) Ibid

(7) Ibid

(8) Bill Fancher and Jenni Parker. "Abortion is Destroying Black America". <u>Catholic Exchange</u> courtesy of Agape Press. September 6, 2004.

(9) Save America Ministries. A Portrait of the Black Family: 2005 V. Accessed December 2, 2006. Found at <http://www.saveus.org/docs/factsheets/portrait_Black_family7-12-05.pdf>

(10) Ibid

(11) The Henry J. Kaiser Family Foundation. <u>HIV/AIDS Policy Fact Sheet</u>. November 2006. <http://www.kff.org/hivaids/upload/3029-071.pdf>

(12) Ibid

(13) Moral Relativism found at www.wikipedia.org

(14) "The Bridge To Gretna: Why Did Police Block Desperate Refugees From New Orleans?" <u>60 Minutes.</u> CBS. 2006. <http://www.cbsnews.com/stories/2005/12/15/60minutes/main1129440.shtml>

(15) Rev. Janine Simpson. "The Urban Initiative". <www.care net.org/publications/cot/UrbanInitiative.pdf> December 2, 2006.

(16) Sanger, Margaret, "A Plan for Peace," <u>The Birth Control Review</u>, April 1932. p. 106.

(17) Ibid.

(18) Delgado, Richard. *The Coming Race War? And Other Apocalyptic Tales of America after Affirmative Action and Welfare*. New York and London .New York University Press, 1996. p. 11-12.

(19) McWhorter, John H. *Losing The Race: Self-Sabotage in Black America*. New York. The Free Press, 2000. p. 27.

(20) Griffin, John Howard. *Black Like Me*. San Antonio, TX. Wings Press, 2004. p. 115.

(21) Elkins, Stanley M. *Slavery: A Problem in American Institutional and Intellectual Life.*The University Library. New York. Grosset & Dunlap, 1963. p. 136.

(22) Ibid. p. 105.

(23) Ebony Pictoral History of Black America: Volume 1 African Past To The Civil War. Nashville, Tennessee. Southwestern Company, 1971. p. 116

(24) Elkins, Stanley M. *Slavery: A Problem in American Institutional and Intellectual Life.* The University Library. New York. Grosset & Dunlap,1963. p.109.

(25) Ibid. p. 109.

(26) Ibid. p. 111.

(27) Ibid. p. 112.

(28) Ibid. p. 113.

(29) Ibid. p. 113.

(30) Ibid. p. 130- 131.

(31) Ibid. p. 130.

(32) Frazier, E. Franklin. <u>The Negro Family in the United States</u>. Notre Dame, Indiana. University of Notre Dame Press, 1939. P. 481.

(33) Woodson, Carter G. <u>The Mis-Education of the Negro</u>. Trenton, NJ. African World Press, Inc, Tenth Edition 1998. p. xiii

(34) Found at www.wikipedia.org.

(35) Kennedy, Stetson. <u>Jim Crow Guide: The Way It Was</u>. Boca Raton. Florida Atlantic University Press, 1959. p. 216-217.

(36) Michael Richards. November 2006. Found at www.youtube.com

(37) Bilbo, Theodore G., Senator. <u>TAKE YOUR CHOICE: Separation or Mongrelization</u> Poplarville, Mississippi. Dream House Publishing Company, 1947 <http://www.churchoftrueisrael.com/tyc/tyc-12.html>

(38) Ibid.

(39) Davis, Thulani. "The Height of Disrespect". <u>Village Voice</u>. March 17-23, 2004.

(40) Pilgrim, David Dr. <u>The Jezebel Stereotype</u>. <http://www.ferris.edu/news/jimcrow/jezebel/>

(41) Davis, Thulani. "The Height of Disrespect". <u>Village Voice</u>. March 17-23, 2004.

(42) Pilgrim, David Dr. <u>The Brute Caricature</u>. Ferris State University. <http://www.ferris.edu/news/jimcrow/brute/>

(43) Du Bois, W.E.B. The Souls of Black Folk. New York. Penguin Books,1989. p. 35.

(44) Locke, Alain. The New Negro: An Interpretation New York: Macmillan, 1925.

(45) Woodson, Carter G. The Mis-Education of the Negro. Trenton, NJ. African World Press, Inc, Tenth Edition 1998. p. 163.

(46) Frazier, E. Franklin. Black Bourgeoisie. New York. Free Press Paperbacks/ Simon & Shuster,1957.p. 129.

(47) Williams, Robert F. A Voice for Black Liberation. Parts I, II, III. <http://whatthepeoplereallythink.com/rwilliams1.htm>

(48) Frazier, E. Franklin. Black Bourgeoisie. New York. Free Press Paperbacks/ Simon & Shuster,1957. p.204.

(49) Ibid. p. 126.

(50) Ibid. p. 168.

(51) Ibid. p. 118.

(52) Frazier, E. Franklin. The Negro Family in the United States. Notre Dame, Indiana. University of Notre Dame Press, 1939. p. 483.

(53) Ibid. p. 485.

(54) Holy Bible: King James Translation. Matthew 16:26.

II. THE ARRESTED DEVELOPMENT OF THE BLACK AMERICAN FEMALE

(1)　White, Deborah Gray. "Female Slaves in the Plantation South ".<u>Before Freedom Came African-American Life in The Antebellum South</u>. Edward D.C. Campbell, Jr. & Kym S. Rice eds. Charlottesville,VA. The Museum of the Confederacy. University Press of Virginia, 1991. p. 103.

(2)　Roberts, James. <u>The Narrative of James Roberts, a Soldier Under Gen. Washington in the Revolutionary War, and Under Gen. Jackson at the Battle of New Orleans, in the War of 1812: "a Battle Which Cost Me a Limb, Some Blood, and Almost My Life"</u>: James Roberts 1753. <www.docsouth.unc.edu/ > CHAPTER VI.

(3)　Willing, Richard. "DNA rewrites history of African Americans". <u>USA Today</u>. January 2, 2006. www.usatoday.com/news/nation/2006-02-01-dna-tests_x.htm.

(4)　Mellon, James ed. <u>BULLWHIP DAYS: The Slaves Remember An Oral History</u>. New York. Weidenfeld & Nicolson,1988. p. 297.

(5)　Ibid. p. 149.

(6)　Kalra, Paul. <u>FROM SLAVE TO UNTOUCHABLE: LINCOLN'S SOLUTION</u> <http://www.ontimemoney.com/FSTU/schapt4/schapt4.htm>

(7)　Ibid.

(8)　Jacobs, Harriet A. <u>Incidents In The Life of a Slave Girl.</u> Yellin, Jean Fagan ed. Cambridge. Harvard University Press,1987. p. 28.

(9) Griffin, John Howard. Black Like Me. San Antonio, TX. Wings Press, 2004. p. 104.

(10) Kennedy, Stetson. Jim Crow Guide: The Way It Was. Boca Raton. Florida Atlantic University Press,1959. p. 61.

(11) Mellon, James ed. BULLWHIP DAYS: The Slaves Remember An Oral History. New York. Weidenfeld & Nicolson,1988. p. 47.

(12) Jacobs, Harriet A. Incidents In The Life of a Slave Girl. Yellin, Jean Fagan ed. Cambridge. Harvard University Press,1987. p. 49.

(13) Mellon, James ed. BULLWHIP DAYS: The Slaves Remember An Oral History. New York. Weidenfeld & Nicolson, 1988. p. 148.

(14) Ibid. p. 296.

(15) Marilyn Yarbrough with Crystal Bennett, "Cassandra and the "Sistahs": the Peculiar Treatment of African American Women in the Myth of Women as Liars" Journal of Gender, Race and Justice .Spring 2000. p. 626-657, 634-655

(16) Ibid.

(17) Scott, David. Lacrosse Players Tout DNA Tests. December 13, 2006. <www.http://apnews.myway.com/article/20061213/D8MO6MS80.html>

(18) Ali, Shahrazad. The Blackman's Guide To Understanding The Blackwoman. Philadelphia. Civilized Publications, 1989. p. 52.

(19) Machiavelli, Nicolò. The Prince. Written c. 1505, published 1515 Translated by W K. Marriott 1908. Rendered into HTML by Jon Roland of the Constitution Society. Chapter XXV.

(20) Leonard. Abigail. W. How Women Pick Mates vs. Flings. January 2, 2007. <www.LiveScience.com>

(21) Ibid.

(22) found at <www.wikipedia.org>

(23) Ibid.

(24) Davis, Thulani. "The Height of Disrespect". Village Voice. March 17-23, 2004

(25) Ali, Shahrazad. The Blackman's Guide To Understanding The Blackwoman. Philadelphia. Civilized Publications,1989. p. 175.

(26) The Ebony Advisor. Ebony Magazine. May 2006.

(27) Morrison, Toni. The Bluest Eye. Middlesex, England. Plume. The Penguin Group, 1994. p. 205.

(28) Holy Bible: King James Translation. Titus 2:3.

(29) Save America Ministries. A Portrait of the Black Family: 2005 Edition. Accessed December 2, 2006. <http://www.saveus.org/docs/factsheets/portrait_Black_family7-12-05.pdf.>

(30) Ibid.

(31) Ibid.

(32) Department of Health Center for Health Statistics. The Health of Minorities in Virginia, 2003. A Report on Vital Events. Richmond: July 2005. p.11- 19.

(33) Ibid.

(34) Ibid

(35) Stokes, Crader, and Smith. <u>Race, Education, and Ferility: A Comparision of Black-White Reproductive Behavior</u>.1977. <www.popcenter.umd.edu/people/derose_laurie/courses/498D_Fall06/Totalfertility.ppt -

(36) Wattenberg, Ben J. <u>Birth Rates Close to Racial Parity</u>. AEI Online. January 1, 2000. <www.http://www.aei.org/publications/pubID.17614/pub_detail.asp>

(37) The Henry J. Kaiser Family Foundation. HIV/AIDS Policy Fact Sheet. http://www.kff.org/hivaids/upload/3029-071.pdf. November 2006

(38) Fears, Darryl."U.S. HIV Cases Soaring Among Black Women". <u>Washington Post.</u> February 7, 2005.

(39) Ibid.

III. THE ARRESTED DEVELOPMENT OF THE BLACK MALE

(1) Farrell, Warren, Phd. <u>The Myth of Male Power</u>. New York. Berkley Books, 1993. p.207

(2) Yellan, Jean Fagan ed. <u>Incidents in The Life of a Slave Girl</u>. Cambridge. Harvard University Press,1987. p.61.

(3) Frazier, E. Franklin. <u>Black Bourgeoisie</u>. New York. Free Press Paper Backs, 1957. p220-221.

(4) Ibid

(5) Pettigrew, Thomas. A Profile of the Negro American. Westport Connecticut. Greenwood Press, 1964. p. 16.

(6) Quigley, Carroll. Tragedy And Hope: A History of The World in our Time. New York. The Macmillan Company, 1966. p.1262.

(7) Ibid. p. 1260-1262

(8) Finkel, David. "The Meaning of Work". Washington Post. Sunday, November 19, 2006.

(9) Tucker, Neely. "Dad, Redefined". Washington Post. Sunday, December 17, 2006.A3.

(10) Pettigrew, Thomas. A Profile of the Negro American. Westport Connecticut. Greenwood Press,1964. p. 18.

(11) Quigley, Carroll. Tragedy And Hope: A History of the world in our Time. New York. The Macmillan Company,1966. p.1262.

(12) Mellon, James ed. BULLWHIP DAYS: The Slaves Remember An Oral History. New York. Weidenfeld & Nicolson,1988. p. 149.

(13) Butterfield, Fox. All God's Children: The Bosket Family and the American Tradition of Violence. New York. Alfred A. Knopf, 1995. p.10

(14) Cole, Jason. "Downside to athleticism". Yahoo! Sports. Decembr 21, 2006.

(15) Griffin, John. Black Like Me. San Antonio, TX. Wings Press, 1960. p. 90.

(16) Battacharya, Sanjiv. "Meet the Mandingos: They're gentlemen in the street, thugs in the bedroom, and your wife's steamiest fantasy," MEN.STYLE.COM. March 16, 2007. found at<http://men.style.com/details/blogs/details/2007/03/the_provocateur.html#more>

(17) Thulani, Davis."The Height of Disrespect," The Village Voice. March 17-23, 2004:1-4

(18) Farrell, Warren, Phd. The Myth of Male Power. New York. Berkley Books, 1993. P.188.

(19) Ibid. p. 58.

(20) Pettigrew, Thomas. A Profile of the Negro American. Westport Connecticut. Greenwood Press. 1964. p. 19.

(21) Ibid. p. 24.

(22) found at <http://www.hrw.org/reports/2001/prison/voices.html>

(23) King. J.L.. On The Down Low. A Journey into the lives of "straight" Black men who sleep with men. New York. Broadway Books, 2004. p. 119.

(24) Ibid. p. 120.

IV. CONSPICIOUS CONSUMPTION

(1) Buffett, Warren. "Berkshire Hathaway Annual Report". March 5, 2006. <http://www.athenaalliance.org/weblog/archives/2005/03/warren_buffett.html>

(2) Crenson, Matt. "GAO Chief Warns Economic Disaster Looms". <u>Associated Press.</u> October 28, 2006. <http://abcnews.go.com/Politics/wireStory?id=2613135&page=2>

(3) Todd Lewan and Dolores Barclay. "Torn From the Land: AP Documents Land Taken From Blacks Through Trickery, Violence and Murder". <u>Associated Press.</u> 2001. <www.seeingBlack.com. >

(4) Woodson, Carter G. <u>The Mis-Education of the Negro.</u> Trenton, NJ. African World Press, Inc.,Tenth Edition 1998. p. 5.

(5) Ibid. p. 48.

(6) Ibid. p. 159.

(7) Frazier, E. Franklin. <u>Black Bourgeoisie</u>. New York. Free Press Paperbacks/ Simon & Shuster,1957. p. 126-127.

(8) Ibid. p. 230.

(9) Ibid. p. 85.

(10) Jones, Charisse. "Life after BET: a billion lessons learned: a cofounder of BET, Sheila C. Johnson became a billionaire when Viacom purchased the network. Now on a new path, she speaks of her disappointments, triumphs and truths". <u>Essence Magazine.</u> May 2005.

(11) <u>Major Realty Firm Accused of Racial Discrimination.</u> August 22, 2006. Found at <www.cbs2chicago.com>

(12) Givhan, Robin. "Bubbly Boycott? Oh Please, Jay-Z, Just Chill". <u>Washington Post</u>. Friday July 7, 2006.

(13) Frazier, E. Franklin. Black Bourgeoisie. New York. Free Press Paperbacks/ Simon & Shuster, 1957. p. 230.

(14) Pettigrew, Thomas F. A Profile of the Negro American. Westport Connecticut. Greenwood Press, 1964. p. 37.

(15) Woodson, Carter G. The Mis-Education of the Negro. Trenton, NJ. African World Press, Inc.,Tenth Edition 1998. p. 104-105.

(16) Ibid. p. 116.

(17) Frazier, E. Franklin. Black Bourgeoisie. New York. Free Press Paperbacks/ Simon & Shuster,1957. p. 234.

(18) Woodson, Carter G. The Mis-Education of the Negro. Trenton, NJ. African World Press, Inc.,Tenth Edition 1998. p. 115.

(19) Ibid.

(20) McWhorter, John H. Losing The Race: Self-Sabotage in Black America. New York. The Free Press, 2000. p. 148.

(21) Frazier, E. Franklin. Black Bourgeoisie. New York. Free Press Paperbacks/ Simon & Shuster,1957. p. 208.

(22) Ibid. p. 199.

(23) Joy, Bill. "Why the future doesn't need us". Wired. August 4, 2000.

(24) Woodson, Carter G. The Mis-Education of the Negro. Trenton, NJ. African World Press, Inc.,Tenth Edition 1998. p.107.

(25) Ibid. p.107.

V. A SPIRITUAL EXODUS

(1) Holy Bible: Amplified Translation. Numbers 11:4-6.

(2) Holy Bible: Amplified Translation. Exodus 14:8-12

(3) Holy Bible: Amplified Translation. Numbers 14:29-33

(4) Holy Bible: King James Translation. 2 Corinthians 10:12

(5) Bilbo, Theodore G., Senator. TAKE YOUR CHOICE: Separation or Mongrelization Poplarville, Mississippi. Dream House Publishing Company, 1947. <http://www.churchoftrueisrael.com/tyc/tyc-12.html>

(6) Holy Bible: King James Translation.1 Corinthians 15:50

(7) <www.http://en.wikipedia.org/wiki/Divinity>

(8) < www.http://en.wikipedia.org/wiki/Hubris>

(9) <www.http://en.wikipedia.org/wiki/Anti-Tom_literature>

(10) Zinn, Howard. A People's History of the United States 1492- Present. New York. Harper Perennial,1995. p. 172.

(11) Faulkner, William. The Collected Stories of William Faulkner. New York. Vintage International/Random House, 1995.

(12) Quigley, Carroll. Tragedy And Hope. A History of The World in our Time. New York. The Macmillan Company,1966.p 1240-1241.

(13) Ibid. p. 1243-1244.

(14) Bergman, Justin. "Valedictorian Debate Sparks Outrage". Associate Press. Washington Times. July 16. 2004.

(15) Holy Bible: Amplified Translation. Exodus 14:8-9.

(16) Golomb, Elan PhD. Trapped in the Mirror. New York: Morrow, pages 19-20. 1992. < www.wikipeidia.org>

(17) Gospel For Asia News Magazine p. 13-14. 2007.

(18) Holy Bible: KING JAMES Translation. Matthew 12:50

(19) Holy Bible: Amplified Translation ACTS 7:35

(20) Holy Bible: Amplified Translation ACTS 7:39

(21) Woodson, Carter G. The Mis-Education of the Negro. Trenton, NJ. African World Press, Inc.,Tenth Edition 1998. p.148.

(22) Holy Bible: KING JAMES Translation. Ezekiel 16:32.

(23) Holy Bible: KING JAMES Translation Exodus 32:8

(24) Holy Bible: KING JAMES Translation Numbers 32:13.

(25) <u>Holy Bible: Amplified Translation.</u> Psalm 95: 10-11.

(26) <u>Holy Bible: Amplified Translation.</u> Hebrews 4:11.

(27) <u>Holy Bible: KING JAMES Translation.</u> Luke 16:15.

Printed in the United States
103171LV00001B/1-99/A